MW01165455

In *Determined Women: The Ostfriesens,* Pat Stuart weaves together the stories of a family of immigrants, particularly of their women whose lives were testaments to the power of determination. What drove them?

"Go to Ostfriesland, and you will understand," Ickka Eilerts Buss would have answered.

Go and you will see a flat swampy fen as good as afloat on the North Sea, a land made so inhospitable by the relentless beating of the waters that for many thousands of years few coveted it enough to invade. Those who did—up to and through the Romans—were sent packing by this race of tall, red-haired people who seemed indifferent to hardship and extremes. They called themselves the Friesii. The free people.

Ickka was an Ostfreisen (East Friesen). She was neither extraordinary nor beautiful; not an intellectual nor particularly talented. But she had the Friesen passion for land and Friesen powers of endurance. Most of all she was determined.

Behrendji DeGroot was beautiful and accomplished but shared Ickka's rocky beginnings as well as her good fortune in marrying up.

What happened? Their story is told here, the two becoming part of a larger picture, their legacy being just one glittering, tiny stone in the great mosaic our ancestors created and called: the American West.

WYBAR HOUSE

Powell, Wyoming, 2015

978-0-9908727-2-6

Cover and interior design by Morrison Creative Company

To Debi Baum without whose dedicated research,
support, and encouragement
this book would never have been written.

ALSO BY PAT A. STUART

Regime Change
Pockets of Magic
Grizzly Memories
A Gathering of Grizzlies

PAT A. STUART

After a thirty-one year career as a CIA operations officer and a shorter period as a horse breeder and exhibiter, Pat A. Stuart reverts back to her interest in history and her undergraduate degree from the University of Oregon to write and research this family memoir. Following her years at Eugene, Pat studied as a Wolcott Scholar at George Washington University, married, and raised a daughter who now has two sons of her own. Pat served tours in Europe, Africa, and the Middle East before retiring to her horse farm in Wyoming, coming full circle back to her childhood haunts. In *Determined Women* she draws on her hugely diverse experiences to paint vivid profiles of the individuals in these books. She sets them into their historical contexts to bring them and their eras to life again.

DETERMINED WOMEN I:

THE OSTFRIESENS

A Family Memoir

PAT A.
STUART

AUTHOR'S NOTE

Determined Women began as a small project, a desire to share a family story. To fill in some details, I contacted Debi Baum for a bit of background material and, gradually, was drawn into the past, looking for an explanation to one question. What made my mother, Marolyn Miller, so single-minded and unstoppable in her determination to build her own cabin as described in the second volume—The New Pioneer?

Did I find the answer? Perhaps. Certainly, the search took me on two journeys—one into the past and into the lives of people previously unknown to me. My second travels were more conventional involving exploration of places and including delightful encounters with family and others who would help me flesh out the stories in the two volumes of *Determined Women*.

While reading, please keep in mind that the spelling of Ostfriesen names varies widely due to the vagaries of individual preferences and historical developments. In addition, surnames and given names have variants that occasionally cause trouble because of naming customs and phonetic spellings. Our Ickka Eilerts Buss was a case in point. She spelled her name variously as Ikke, Ickke, and Ickka. Since her name is pronounced 'Ick.kah,' I chose the latter spelling rather than the most common one, Ikke, which seems as though it would be pronounced 'Eye.key.'

But however the spelling goes, it's the stories that count. I hope you enjoy reading *Determined Women* as much as I enjoyed writing it.

February 2015

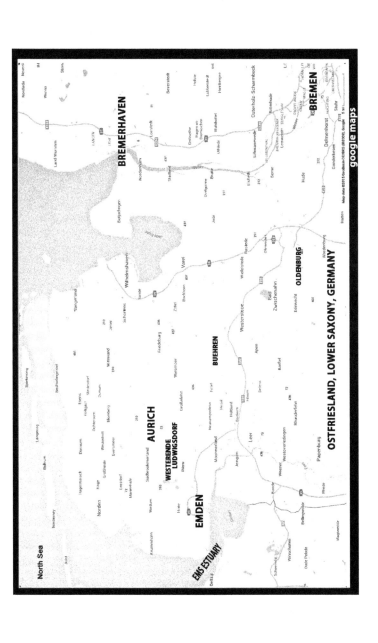

OSTFRIESLAND, LOWER SAXONY, GERMANY

Wir wollen bleiben frie und friesisch.
We want to stay free and Friesen.

CONTENTS

THE BUSS FAMILY LINEAGE

Berend Gerdes (1687-1727) m. 1707 Ancke Gerdes (1687-1723)

Gerd Behrends (1708-1785) m. 1733 Else Catharina Janssen (1709-1782)

Hinrich Gerdes Buss (1740-1810) m. 1764 Gesche Siemering (1743-1811)

Gerd Berends Buss (1777-1843) m. 1801 Elshe Catharina Flesner (1777-1838)

Tette Christina m. 1802 Martens Flesner
Hinrich Gerdes m. 1805 Gretje Tholen
Weert Gerdes m. 1814 Ahrendji Ubben
m. Maria Paeben
Gesche Gerdes m. 1835 Gerd Franken
Jann Gerdes m. 1822 Ickka Geddes Eilerts

Gerhard   Elsche C.   Janna   Heinrich   Johann   Janna   Gesche   Weert   Eilert
         | m. 1868 Christoph Müller

Lena   Maria   Ida   Herma   Bertha   Johann   Bernhard   Gesina   Walter   Elmer (Willie)
                                                                           | m. Ethel Smith

PART ONE
OSTFRIESLAND

*"Go to Ostfriesland and you will understand. It is the
land and the sea that shape us."*

The Buss home in Ludwigsdorf built in 1808. (From "*The Buss Family of Ostfriesland*" by Debi Baum and the collection of Helmut Barberg. Courtesy of Marten Hagan and Blanche Hosfeldt.)

1
1838, Westerende, Ostfriesland, Hannover, Germany

She was like one of the sparks flying upwards from the bonfire, weightless, rising into the night sky, mesmerized by the sound of strings and drums, by the beating of clogs on bare earth. Strands of hair had escaped from under her mop cap, competing with the flaring brilliance of the firelight. Around her other girls danced with their young men. Older men lounged against walls or on benches, mugs in hand, talking of the affairs of the day, of Victoria who had inherited Hannover and, thus, Ostfriesland. Salic law, everyone was saying, made her rule illegal. A woman emperor? Impossible. "It can't last," they agreed. "The Hannoverians will choose a new king."

So I imagine that May Day of 1838 in the village of Westerende, west of Aurich, on the edge of the North Sea. The beer flowed, the music worked its magic around the village May Pole—a tall Birch profusely and profanely decorated with green branches and paper flowers. On Sunday the people would trail soberly into church. But on this one night of the year they whirled and stomped and celebrated the coming of spring and the renewed fertility of earth and its creatures. Urges suppressed for 364 days surfaced. There was a reason that the mid-wife had to rush from house to house in February.

Ickka Eilerts would be seventeen in a month, and it's likely she could cavort with the best of them. Her nubile and muscular flesh sat comfortably on a straight back and long, strong legs capable of carrying her through the entire night of festivities. Hair with red highlights, parchment white skin, and blue eyes contrasted with the deep blues and dark browns of the surrounding night, creating a portrait worthy of a Flemish painter—a van Dyck or Rubens.

Was boat captain Jann Gerdes Buss of Ludwigsdorf, a hamlet a bit more than a mile away, one of her partners that May Day? It's possible. In fact he may have spent quite a bit of time in Westerende given the proximity of the village's moorings—a widened place on the big canal connecting Aurich with the port of Emden—to his home. Plus, he probably had relatives among Ickka's neighbors.

Even so, to expect marriage between someone like Jann and a girl like Ickka would have been a stretch.

Jann, while still a working man, owned his own boat plus several parcels of land. He had excellent prospects, and at twenty-six was very likely more than a bit full of himself having never known want or hardship, having been the youngest child in a prosperous, loving home and probably denied very little. In short he was a real marital catch, turning the heads of village girls and their mothers as he sailed Ostfriesland's canal highways.

In sharp contrast, Ickka's father was firmly settled near the bottom of the Friesen social structure, a place of no particular expectations but at the same time of no shame. It was a status he shared with the majority of Ostfriesens. "That which doesn't kill you, strengthens you," might have been his motto. Gerd Eilerts was a survivor from a long line of survivors.

Family histories refer to Gerd as a *warfman* and a *colonist*. To be a *warfman* meant to own a small holding (probably an acre or less) and a house. As a *colonist,* he hired out to earn a living, probably doing a bit of farming, peat cutting, land draining—all the hard, physical labor of the time and place. In a good year he would earn enough to feed and clothe his family. In a bad year?

No matter. In a Europe with still a decade or more to go before the dragging skirts of feudalism would disappear, Gerd Eilerts would have considered himself a free man, not a serf or peasant. He was not bound to someone else's land but owned his own. In principle, he lived where he wanted, moved where he would, and had a say in local matters. The hard reality, though, was that a man's economic situation governed what he could and could not do. Overpopulation, land scarcity and a subsistence economy imposed its own reality, dividing the people into classes which for the most part kept those at the bottom locked in a cycle of near penury. While they could move about physically, seeking work where they could find it, there was barely more hope for them of social mobility than there was for a serf in the Rhineland who was permanently tied to his master's land and service.

In the months after that May Day, Jann left no record of having Ickka on his mind. He definitely did have other concerns.

All was not well at home. His parents were both in their sixties, and his mother was declining. As the youngest of Gerd Berens Hinrichs Buss and Elsche Catharina Janssen Flesner's five children, Jann was the last at home, but all of his siblings lived within an hour's walk of Ludwigsdorf. Both daughters had been given their dowries and dwelled with their in-laws. Hinrichs, the oldest son, had his own farm near Ihlowerfehn with a wife who'd borne him nine children. Weert had recently moved with his new wife, Ahrendji, to a small farm.

For a few more months lucky Jann could always plead the demands of business to duck helping his father. He could stroll whistling to his boat's moorings and sail away, leaving his parents and his problems behind. In September 1838, though, with Elsche Catharina terminally ill the situation came to a head.

Perhaps as part of a deal to secure their own care, the old folks turned over their house and about three acres to Jann and Weert. A month later, Mother Elsche Catharina died, and Weert and Ahrendji returned to the family home. Presumably, the idea was that Ahrendji would care for both her father-in-law and the household.

This arrangement lasted no more than three months. Immediately after the Christmas season of 1838, Jann bought Weert's share of their final bit of patrimony. Weert and a pregnant Ahrendji immediately moved out of the ancestral home, returning to their own little farm, leaving Jann the sole owner of a comfortable and relatively new house and its acreage in addition to his boat and other holdings. He also had the sole care of his father.

Now, someone had to build the fires and keep them burning. There were meals to prepare, water to carry, linen to wash and dry, rooms to be cleaned, and a myriad of other essential daily chores.

How to manage when Jann's primary source of income kept him moving around the country, often away from home for days at a time?

His obvious solution was to marry. Yet, Jann still showed no signs of proposing. At least not to Ickka.

Possibly he expected his sister, Gesche, who lived almost next door, to step in and manage the household. And he may have had good reason to think she would. Gesche (who would eventually come to America with Jann) had lived at home and cared for their parents and her brothers until she was twenty-six. Then she accepted the offer of a 34-year-old from nearby Ihlowerfehn. Gerd Franken.

Theirs was an uneven situation—a match between an old maid with a good dowry and a poor boy. Gerd Franken was a day laborer who barely earned enough to feed his elderly parents (both in their seventies). How would he ever support an expanding family? But he was available, and Gesche faced the fast-arriving day when her brothers would bring home wives who would supplant her position of authority in the Buss home. For his part, Gerd needed a caregiver. And, there was Gesche's dowry to consider.

They married and, once the ceremony was over, the newlyweds and the older Frankens settled in Ludwigsdorf, likely into a house the bride's father provided as part of her dowry. Likely, too, Gerd Franken was kept employed by one or the other of the Buss males.

Thus, Gesche was nearby and beholden to her family. But in this New Year's season she had her own troubles—had just buried her father-in-law, was encumbered with a grieving mother-in-law, had a husband, a toddler, and a nursing infant, and was endlessly busy feeding and clothing all of her charges on the poor wages her husband earned.

It takes no imagination to hear what she would've had to say to her baby brother if he'd solicited her unpaid help. A disbelieving, "You want what … ? Are you out of your pea-sized, spoiled little mind!" Or words or looks to that effect. His elder sister with a large family of her own would've given him even shorter shift.

It's probable, therefore, that Jann ended up hiring a village woman to make meals and clean for his father. And, there—one way or the other—he was. Paying for work that a wife, if he only had one, would do for the price of her food. Plus, a wife could be expected to do so much more. That's if all he wanted was the usual combination of household drudge, breeding machine, and farm worker. If so, he could've married immediately and saved himself fourteen months of coping. No. Jann seems to have been looking for something more.

We know he was uncomfortably situated between social classes, a not uncommon place to be when societal mores are in flux. And, Jann clearly had expectations. How not? He had spent a lifetime traveling—first with his father, then on his own. He'd met and done business with men from the world over, giving him knowledge and a touch of sophistication foreign to the average prosperous village lad. Yet, his book learning was rudimentary; his language skills undeveloped—he spoke the Plattdeutsch of his people. His Hochdeutsch (spoken by the church and business communities) would have been accented. His French, the lingua franca of the upper classes, was probably at a survival level as was his English. And the biggest impediments to his upward social mobility? He had no inherited status and worked with his hands.

Even considering these negatives, Jann would've passed many pleasant and educational hours dealing with prosperous merchants of Emden and Aurich. He'd likely been inside their homes and exposed to the comforts and luxuries of the well-to-do. More relevant, he'd met their daughters. Had he dined and danced with these fashionably dressed young ladies with their perfumes from Paris and their fabrics from the Orient? Had he formed an attachment to one of them or to the dowry one of them would bring? Did he see himself married to a woman of accomplishment, happy presiding over a table set with linen and silver?

Jann was still young enough to have his dreams as well as his ambitions. Besides, he was now the owner of a good-sized house (even if it was in a very small village), of many acres of land, and of his own prosperous haulage business. Surely, he was a solid marital catch. That was no dream.

But young men often have their fondest desires thwarted. The year, 1839, could not have been a good one for Jann. The loving home he'd known in Ludwigsdorf had vanished with his mother. His house was often cold; his father bereft without his life's partner whom he clearly had loved. Then, although Jann's shipping business seems to have been doing well, things came to a head during the Christmas season. Perhaps Jann proposed and was turned down by the girl of his choice? Whatever happened, shortly thereafter he contracted to marry Ickka Eilerts.

Did he begin the process on New Year's Eve of 1840, walking to Westerende for *spek un dikken* or "bacon and pancakes?" Why imagine that particular day? Because New Year's Eve had evolved into a day for lovers among the Ostfriesens. Women looking for husbands would prepare special bacon pancakes, one containing seven *speks* (pieces of bacon). If the man of her dreams appeared, she'd make sure he got that particular pancake as a sign of true love. Then, too, girls could take the initiative and invite the man to her house to drink beer and share her bacon pancakes. If she chose, she could even propose to him.

As he skirted small fields and crossed drainage ditches, Jann had to be supremely confident Ickka's father would accept his suit, for the Eilerts girl would bring nothing to the marriage except herself. This ruled her out as a match for most men of property ... well, to be blunt about it ... men without the need to combine nurse, cook, house servant, farm hand, and wife in one package.

Nor was she beautiful or alluring, although her face was a long, pleasing oval, her complexion rouged by exposure, her nose a bit thick but well-proportioned, and her lips generous and full. With a different upbringing, her eyes might have made her beautiful, but even at eighteen they wore, for the most part, a hard determined look which in time would become almost fierce and definitely riveting.

As Jann strode along, he would've seen other men out and about on the same errand. They would know exactly what he was doing. Passing each other or walking along together, they exchanged ribald jokes and engaged in the universal sexual banter of young men seeking mates.

Whenever he went, upon arrival Jann would've scraped the mud from his clogs before entering the Eilerts' home, which probably consisted only of one room in which the family slept, ate, dressed, processed and prepared food and clothing, occasionally bathed, and worked. Bending his head to pass under the low lintel, he would've had to squint to see in the hut's smoky dim interior. But even that could not disguise the poverty within, for the Eilerts' home was little more than a mud and wattle structure built on an ancient model, sufficient to keep the elements somewhat at bay but offering little comfort. Worse to twenty-first century noses and perhaps to Jann's as well, it smelled of poverty—of sweat, of urine-soaked reeds and manure moldering in the attached animal byre, of wet and well-seasoned woolens and the nearby cesspit. No doubt but Janna and Ickka Eilerts worked diligently to keep their home and those in it clean, but their lack of resources, the crush of bodies, the chamber pot, and the demands of just staying alive made that difficult to impossible.

Yet, there were pleasant fragrances, too, of burning peat mixed with the rich odor of wet peat and clay earth in the fields.

And, the background sounds were soothing, relaxing. The big canal that passed the village washed its banks as it always did. Winter rain may have pattered on puddles, plopped off the bundled roof reeds and, as an occasional gust of wind caught a shower, it splattered drops against the cottage's north side. The poultry and whatever animals the Eilerts might've been fortunate enough to own that year would've stirred in their rude lean-to under the Eilerts' roof.

Whatever the date of the visit, Jann Buss and Gerd Eilerts would have drawn their stools close to the hearth and held their beer mugs in big, callused hands, while they talked of larger affairs, perhaps of the railroad that now connected Amsterdam to Haarlem and of how extending the rail lines would affect the canal boat business. As the day faded outside, the room darkened and the glow of the burning peat softened their hard features.

Finally, having covered all of the important matters, with fresh mugs of beer to lubricate their discussion, they would have gotten down to business, ticking off the essential points. Like:

"I can think of no family connection in my lifetime," Gerd might have said. A check of church records was a required step in the run-up to a wedding because Ostfriesens generally only married other Ostfriesens and bloodlines had become confused over the past several thousand years. No consanguinity within three generations was the rule.

Next, there was the question of pregnancy. Unlike in almost every other part of Europe, many Ostfriesen families still placed greater value on proof of fecundity than on the dubious benefits of a virgin bride. Jann, exposed as he had been to other ways of thinking, might've been a bit put off by this. At any rate we know Ickka did not enter the marriage with an existing pregnancy.

The rest of the exchange was predictable. No dowry was offered and none expected. Ickka could take nothing to a marriage but the clothes on her back, her two muscular legs and two strong arms. The only question left was one of timing.

After Jann's departure, Gerd might have closed the wooden shutters against the night and whatever moisture dripped beyond the ample eaves and sat back down to finish his beer and stare at the fire. Janna and Ickka would have continued their chores while the younger children, probably banished during the visit to huddle in the animal byres, would've crept back inside.

Given the proximity of their villages, Gerd would've known all there was to know about the Buss family of Ludwigsdorf. So, he may well have sat brooding over how Jann's father had made his money sailing his boats on the local canals and, some said, even crossing the sea to trade in England. He would know about how Gerd and Elsche Catharina had built their house and, together, carved their initials in a beam. He would have heard how the two had prospered and provided for all of their children.

Gerd, thinking of all of this, could hope that Jann was a chip off the old block. He could hope that Jann would make Ickka a decent if not loving husband. Whatever, Gerd would have concluded that the marriage would be a good one, if not for his daughter then for his grandsons. None of Ickka's boys would ever have to take to the road with their scythes on their backs, hoping to find work cutting hay. No. At this point in his thoughts, Gerd could be excused for feeling a bit bitter since he had no idea how his own sons would thrive, yet alone survive as adults.

There was no question of Ickka's refusal, of course. Despite the charming customs with the Sadie Hawkins-type day and the bacon pancakes, girls were expected to do as they were told.

Gerd would have taken her cooperation for granted. Nor is he likely to have discussed the subject with his wife.

So, how did Mother Janna feel about the whole thing? Proud, perhaps, and happy she would have bragging rights in the village, but otherwise not so good. After years spent training the girl, Janna would lose her labor. And Ickka at the peak of her performance! Just when her help was such a godsend in caring for the younger ones?

Then, what about Ickka? What thoughts passed through her practical mind as she did her work and eavesdropped on the men? The material advantages were obvious, of course, but mostly they meant she'd have more space to clean, a bigger garden and more animals to tend and no one to help her. She could've had no illusions that Jann would lavish clothes or money or luxuries on her. That would never happen.

But marriage to him had one big plus: She was going to a house with no other women … just the married sister living in the same village. Unlike most girls whose husbands moved them into the family home and who became little better than a slave to the other women of the house, Ickka would be her own mistress. Well. Slave to her husband and his father first; slave to everything else second. But she could make her own schedule and run her own affairs however she liked. As long as the work got done, her husband and father-in-law could not complain. Could they?

But where was love or romance in this equation? Did Ickka pine for another? Was she infatuated with Jann? Possibly, but in her world the idea of "romantic love" and "happily ever after" were abstract concepts existing in ballads and old stories of princes and princesses. In her world if a girl married a toad, he stayed a toad. Perhaps, though, she might have mused, what about a headstrong, egocentric, opinionated boy/man like Jann? He might grow up. He might even come to have some affection for her? Or so any girl might hope.

Lust and sexual arousal was another matter. Whether or not she'd had sexual encounters, given her care of livestock and her proximity to her parents' coupling, she knew exactly what to expect of that aspect of marriage.

How would Jann be in bed? His hands were large and strong, his body muscular and athletic. On the other hand, Ickka may well have found her mind wandering from sex to the luxury of having a real bed and her own quilts and sharing them with just one other person. The prospect of sleeping warm could well have stirred her more than the thought of the man in bed next to her. She would have to wait and see about that.

Certainly, Jann Buss was as close as she could ever expect to find to a dream husband. But Ickka was never one to delude herself, and she would not have done so then. Jann needed an unsalaried laborer. He would expect her to work as hard as she did in her father's house. Otherwise, why marry her?

Silent and thinking her own thoughts, the girl would've had no time on the evening of her affiancing to either celebrate or mourn her fate but would've been expected to keep working, possibly carding wool while sitting on a stool near the fire with her skirt, which would have been far from voluminous, tucked about her bare ankles. Besides dress, a shift, and apron, she would've worn a pair of wooden shoes and a knit wool shawl. Then, too, women and girls generally sported a plain, snood-like cap of home-made linen that reached from their foreheads to the nape of their necks.

Did she possess stockings or gloves, overcoat or nightgown, "small" garments or hats? We don't know, but we can assume she made do with a heavy shawl for winter and a prettier one for church plus a ribbon to match. She would also have made herself a proper bonnet that tied under the chin, perhaps even have edged it in lace scraps and made a matching handkerchief to tuck in her bodice for Sundays and festivals. She would never have known or worn much better.

Her earliest memories would've been of working alongside her mother, perhaps of being slapped when her little hands dropped a bucket or for crying when her stomach was empty or her bones frozen with cold. In the winter her nose ran, her hands and feet developed chilblains, and her body itched from fleas and lice. When her head ached, which would probably have been often, she had no recourse but to ignore the pain and keep working. Pain, as she no doubt learned in church, was a human's lot. Pain let you know you were still alive. And, it could always be worse.

To be poor and Ostfriesen was to have a deep understanding of deprivation and hardship, because it often was worse. Ickka had yet to experience just how much.

2
Ostfriesland—The Land and its People

Theirs was not so much a land as a flat, **flat**, flat swampy fen, as good as afloat on the North Sea. In this place, you could see as far as mist and fog would let you with only imperceptible slopes to the ground and few trees to interrupt any line of sight. The views were in greens and grays, seen through heavy fogs, disconcerting mists, and watery sunlight. From above on a sunny day, Ostfriesland appeared a lacy-edged plate of variegated jade dropped between land and sea, its rich soapy tones reflected by the sky—the canals like veins traced in stone.

For centuries, the people lived safe on their remote hammocks, the sea washing their feet and sometimes submerging their fires, sending them into their boats. Gradually they wrested small holdings from the sea, and by the nineteenth century Ostfriesland consisted of several zones. One was of small islands, sand bars, and hammocks, the latter called "warfs," which were connected to the mainland during low tide; isolated otherwise. Behind this zone were the dikes, built and maintained through the centuries to hold back the sea from the bog and swampland which formed much of the remainder of the country. Where these had been drained, there were farms.

One thing about living in such an inhospitable place, Ostfriesens felt protected from human predations by the treacherous sailing conditions of the sea to the north and the way armies bogged down, literally, when trying to invade from the south. In fact, territorially ambitious neighbors could reach them only via the River Ems on the west and a narrow strip of high ground connecting to Hannover on the east.

No one knows when or how the Friesii—who would separate into East, West, and North Friesens—settled on the North Sea. Archeological finds show people there four thousand years back. The Romans left the first inscribed record of them, noting a fierce tribe of big-bodied, blue-eyed, red-maned warriors unable to bear heat or thirst but inured to cold and deprivation, men who had a system of chieftaincy which rested on discussion and group consensus. Their very name came from the Goth word for free.

In their push north, the Romans first negotiated tribute from the Frisii. Later, when the "free" people refused to pay, they sent their legions to punish and collect. It was a disaster for the legions and, after that, Rome left the tribe alone. Most would-be conquerors did in those centuries. Fussing with the Friisi was too much trouble for too little gain. Why bother.

Change, thus, came slow to the Frisii and Christianity even slower. They were Odinists and happy with their beliefs long after all of the other Northern European tribes had converted. When they did succumb to the priests on the heels of Charlemagne's armies, the pace of change increased.

The emperor not only solidified the Christian church in their lives but codified their legal practices, which rested on "the will of the people." Such had been their practice for as long as any story told, their most common assertion being, *Wir wollen bleiben frie und friesisch* or "We want to stay free and Friesen." Charlemagne's version of this was called the Lex Frisonium.

In one way or another, the Ostfriesens generally did remain *frie*, governing themselves through a system of elected judges. While elsewhere in Europe the tribes intermingled, lost their identities, and were reduced to serfdom, Ostfriesens—locked in their watery lands—retained their identity and remained for the most part "free and Friesen."

Which is not to say that they did not occasionally play minor roles on the larger European stage. Friesens spent a few hundred years using their sea skills to profit as pirates and marauders of one sort or another, their way of life bringing them into armed combat with other coastal peoples. Mostly, they fought the Saxons, but in one period they allied with their Saxon enemies to invade Britain, many of the Friesii remaining in England where the Friesen tongue became a major element in a new language— Old English.

Then, despite a huge and impressive dike-building effort, a series of great storm floods inundated their already watery lands in 1164, 1334, and 1362. For a time the majority of Ostfriesens took themselves off to Kent, England, to live among a people whose language had its roots in their own and where they felt comfortable. Some stayed as their distant ancestors had, but others returned to Ostfriesland when the waters receded.

These disasters and dislocations opened the way to the establishment again of chieftaincies, not on the feudal model but on an older Germanic one based on clans, a system that still left the people largely free and with local home rule. Gradually, though, that yielded to a period of chieftaincies … the country being divided into a dozen small pieces. Then came a reunification but under external rule, Ostfriesland being awarded first to one capitol then to another until people joked, "It's Saturday. Our taxes go to London."

Rule from outside, no matter from Berlin, Hannover, Paris or London, lay with varying degrees of severity on the people in their remote, watery fens. Where necessary, they adapted. In the matter of religion, many converted happily from Catholicism to

Lutheranism, finding Martin Luther's manifestos in sync with their basic thinking. A man, for instance, should have his own copy of the Bible and should be able to read it for himself. Church schools and basic literacy for both men and women became a part of everyone's lives thereafter and every home eventually had a Bible.

In the matter of language, as another example, the people retained their Friesen tongue for many centuries before it was squeezed out by the regionally dominant Plattdeutsch (a Germanic tongue spoken in the low-lying regions along the North Sea). Plattdeutsch in turn had a grammar and vocabulary strongly influenced by Old English. And, as we've seen, Old English had been formed in part from 5th century Friesen. It was all very circular.

In time the people also began to learn Prussian German or High German, using it in the courts and churches, their children exposed to it first in church schools and, more recently, in government-funded schools. Through it all, almost to the present, the people continued speaking Low German at home.

One big, imposed change occurred during the Napoleonic era. Conquerors had found it extremely difficult to administer a people who used a patronymic system of naming—the first name of a father becoming in its plural form the last name of each of his children, the last name thus changing through the generations. How could you keep track of such people?

Napoleon didn't try. He mandated that every family adopt a surname. Some people complied, some didn't … at least not immediately. A surname was like an identity card. It marked you and branded you and made you easier for someone else to control. But eventually even the most recalcitrant holdouts were drawn into the system.

The imposition of surnames also made it easier for governments to collect taxes and harder for the people to avoid conscription. All Ostfriesens evaded the tax collector where they could; paid when they couldn't. They tried hard to stay out of other men's wars—wars that never seemed to stop in Europe—and preferred to pay bounties to capitols like Berlin than allow conscription of their young men.

To pay you have to earn, and Ostfriesland offered its people little in the form of economic resources. They knew what was to be known about the North Sea, of course, and many men in every generation made their living on its waters. Better, the bogs yielded peat, which came to be in demand across Europe. Otherwise, they only had the land they created.

The land. The constant struggle to acquire land, the need to claw it inch by inch out of bog and swamp, the relentless struggle with the sea … all of these realities of life in Ostfriesland stamped its people, built into the genetic code a lust for land. Only the land could give a man and his family security. Only land and more land could ensure survival.

Thus, Ostfriesens became known not just for their skills as sailors, boat builders, and fishermen, but as farmers and as breeders of cattle and horses—the Friesen cow, the Friesen horse, and lighter built Ostfriesen horse all being in demand across Europe.

Among the more practically important aspects of land holding in Ostfriesen society were inheritance customs. Few would dream of breaking up painfully acquired property among heirs. Instead, a man selected one from among his offspring to inherit. While this was not a universal rule, it was a practical one, ensuring that at least one member of each generation owned a useable farm. Unfortunately, it left many young men with no alternative but day labor (when they could find it) and meant young women either found husbands, went into service, or prostituted their bodies. Women had no rights and only basic literacy. Ickka, herself, learned enough to read simple Bible verses, sign her own name, and count.

She also learned her place. In mid-nineteenth century Ostfriesland, women had about the same value as any other chattel. For the most part, they accepted this as their God-designated lot in life, immutable and fixed. "What can't be cured, must be endured," they said and got about the important work of raising their children and feeding their families. Yet, opposition to their men could flare and, when it did, the men sometimes listened, sometimes struck the woman down—unless she decked him first.

Violence was not uncommon; tempers ran close to the surface. In this land of extremes where the sea might rise unexpectedly and breach a dike, where canals laboriously dredged one day could silt in the next, where families watched helplessly as their houses washed away, men took out their sense of powerlessness on their women and each other. Women either suffered or gave as good as they got.

This was the context in which Ickka grew up. This was the land and the sea that created a a woman who was going to need every one of the survival mechanisms built into her DNA by several thousand years of experience and trained into her psyche by her tough upbringing—starting with her marriage.

And, so, the banns were posted, the marriage words were said, accompanied no doubt by copious quantities of beer. The villagers and Jann's friends may have held the usual chivaree, stealing the bride from her marriage bed.

Here, Ickka's testing began.

3
Ickka's Marriage

If Ickka couldn't see herself in silks and satins, how did she perceive her place in life? As lucky? Most probably. She had a solid roof over her head, enough food to eat, only two men to care for and, best of all, she was soon pregnant. Jann's father, the man she'd been married to nurse, probably was something of a burden. The rest of her workload, though, while onerous by twenty-first century standards, was routine and expected. Plus, no matter how temperamental her husband, he was gone on his boat a good portion of the time, leaving her with a huge workload but an amazing amount of independence and, best of all, she was pregnant.

As her belly swelled, her eyes probably softened in secret pleasure, momentarily showing a glimpse of the girl she might have been with a different upbringing. For the first time in her life, she could look forward to having something of her own, a child she could love unreservedly, a life she could shape and nurture.

Ickka wasn't the only one to be happy about the child, of course. In such a tightknit community everyone would take pleasure in the coming of a new child, in this proof that the young wife was fertile and the husband virile, in the prospect of another life to guarantee the survival of all. Among people so close to the land and living on the edge of subsistence, there could never be too many children.

The baby was born in November to a house fragrant with

the smell of burning peat, yet with brick walls damp and cold from early winter storms. It was a boy, a small package of priceless humanity. You could marvel at fingernails and toenails, identical miniatures of their father and mother's. You could put your finger against his shell-like palm and his fingers might close on yours. He was a miracle.

Jann's sisters and their husbands certainly hurried to the house the day after the birth along with the better part of the village of Ludwigsdorf to share in the joy and witness the baptism. Ickka's mother, Janna Eilerts, would have skirted the fields to be there. Her father and siblings might have come, as well.

Ickka, though confined to bed, would have prepared everything necessary before her labor began, but it was up to Janna, Tette Christiana, and Gesche to load the table with the butter bread, the sausages and cheeses and for Jann to fill a mug for each guest. Gerd Franken no doubt helped where he could. If Ickka's father, Gert Eilerts, came, he probably made himself comfortable with a mug of strong drink.

The women wrapped the little boy in the Buss family christening gown. Then with light from candles and fire brightening the interior of the house, the Lutheran parish priest spoke the words of welcome to the boy and sprinkled him with holy water, naming him Gerd Gerhard Janssen Buss. He didn't cry.

Three days later he took one last breath and passed from this world. This time it was just the women who came to the house, their faces dolorous and grim but determined, too. They washed and clothed the tiny body with Ickka looking on, eyes scratchy with grief, her breasts unused. Later in the day the pathetically small coffin came from the carpenter's shop, and Gerd Gerhard

Janssen Buss was placed inside.

Again, Jann filled mugs of beer, this time for those who had helped in the final preparations. Then, they carried the infant to lie in a churchyard plot Jann had bought for his family. The church bell tolled while, back in Ludwigsdorf, Ickka turned her head into her blankets. She had warmth, she had enough to eat, she had security. She had to remember what she had, not what she'd lost.

As for Jann, life had dealt him his second major blow. For twenty-six years, any disappointments he'd suffered had been minor. Now, within the short space of two years, he'd sustained two major set-backs. Did he suck it up and put on as good a face as possible? Or did he sulk; sail off on his boat. Worse, did he blame Ickka and take his frustration out on her? In the future, he would make decisions that showed complete disregard for the health and safety of Ickka and her children. Did the attitude that allowed such acts have its origins in these days?

Otherwise once buried and gone, the short life of Gerd Gerhard Janssen Buss had created only the slightest of ripples in the emotional climate of Ludwigsdorf. These things happened. Child mortality was high. Which fact didn't make the reality any easier for Ickka, who had to endure not just the loss of her child but the platitudes rained on her by the village women who at the same time were probably giving her sideways glances. After all, who could be blamed for the loss of a child but the mother? Was Ickka only going to give birth to sickly children?

Jann wasn't the only one likely to think the baby's death was Ickka's fault.

Another thing. The Buss and Eilerts families were non-demonstrative people when it came to showing either sympathy or affection. There would've been no physical comfort for Ickka, no hand held in compassion, no arm around the shoulder for support. Even if Ickka had taken the walk to the grave in the churchyard, she would've marched solo, the mourners keeping careful inches between their bodies, not even their sleeves touching. But Ickka hadn't made that walk. With her week's mandatory confinement far from over, she'd have missed the closure of a burial.

Possibly, Jann's sister, Gesche, who was ten years older than Ickka but who had two boys of her own, was a comfort of sorts. Tette Christiana, even older, would have brought covered dishes. Maybe her mother, too, came to sit with her. And maybe not. After all, Ickka's grief was such a common thing, was 'a woman's lot,' was a question of: "No point in encouraging her to wallow in her grief. The sooner she learns to live with it, the better off she'll be."

And life did move on. Ickka didn't get pregnant again for another year but allowing a year between pregnancies was normal. In the meantime the house, her ailing father-in-law, and the land around the house had their own imperatives. Ickka would have had a truck garden and, though it was dormant during the most intense period of her inner mourning, there was the inevitable winter work of clearing and maintenance. Then came plowing, harrowing, planting, weeding, harvesting, and preserving. More, there was no moratorium on caring for the old man and the farm animals—for the beasts who lived under the same roof with her. No matter what else happened, they had to be fed, watered, doctored and tended—brought in during bad weather and let out during good.

Every day she swept and, likely, scrubbed the tile floors of the house Jann's parents had built, passing under the beam on which the two had carved their initials to remind subsequent generations of the partnership that had produced the house and its occupants. As rain streamed over the windows outside, Ickka did her chores inside.

Jann might have helped with the seasonal work, taking the cow to a bull for breeding or to the butcher for slaughter. He might also have done some farming in those first years, but then again, since there was more profit in his canal transport business, much of the farm work would have been left to the wife; some of it farmed out to hired laborers like his brother-in-law, Gerd Franken. Then as Jann invested his transport profits in land and his farm holdings grew, he might have leased one of his plots to Gerd or to other landless men for a percentage of their crop yields or for a fixed annual payment.

Ickka would have done the rest of the work, seeing that the sow and the ewes were bred and the roosters and ganders doing their jobs. She would also midwife births, sheer sheep and clean and card their wool. Her days would have been full of smoking and drying meat, rendering lard and making soap, helping in the harvests then drying or pickling and preserving its products. The butchering of the big animals was probably handled by a man who made his living at slaughtering, gutting, hanging the meat to cure and tanning the hides. Grain went to the mill for grinding, the job of transporting it managed by Jann or a hired man.

On a daily basis, Ickka would clean manure from the barn which was at one end of the house. She would feed slop to the pigs, fork hay to the cattle and sheep, spread grain for the fowl. She would butcher out the smaller animals and birds for food, processing fur, hair, hides, and feathers. Every day the cow needed milking, the milk separating. Once a week she would churn butter and bake bread. Some days hooves from butchered animals would fill the big pot hanging over the fire, water surrounding them gradually turning to jelly or glue. Other days the pot would hold buckwheat on its way to becoming a thick beer. While she kept the fire hot enough to simmer whatever liquid was in her pot, she cleaned long tubes of guts, or chopped up sweet meats to fill sausage casings.

Ickka's hands were busy from pre-dawn to dark, the seasons driving her tasks.

Not to forget, there were Jann's siblings and extended family and all of the familial obligations that came with name days and christenings of other women's babies, of marriages and funerals, of holiday meals and church festivals. As women had come to help her during her confinement, she would go to their aide, would dress babies for christenings or wash them for their funerals. There were dishes and gifts to be made and taken to the homes of neighbors in their times of celebration or grief. There was the parish priest to invite to dinner and Sunday suppers to prepare for whomever Jann brought home, mostly family.

Family. The village was, in fact, one large extended family with everyone related in multiple ways to everyone else. Ostfriesens discouraged marriage outside the larger Ostfriesen gene pool and had been in-breeding since long before the Romans made the first written account of their society. Everyone was family. "Your business is your business and no one else's," people said. Except it didn't work that way because everyone you knew was somehow related to you. Thus, it was best to stay informed. Who knew when your neighbors' problems might spill over and become yours? And, another 'besides,' what else was there to talk about but each other?

Fascinating stuff, gossip. The substance of life. Men smoked, sat in the pubs or before their own fires, and kept each other informed—they didn't call it gossip—in the late evenings. Women chatted with sisters, aunts, cousins, and mothers over cook pots and to neighbors across garden fences as they weeded. Then, there was quilting. It was one of a woman's major pleasures.

Quilting. It was such a relief to have a reason to sit in company with other women, hands busy, voices active. This was one of the few female chores done best by a team and it was a job, not the folk art/recreational pastime it has become. Blankets were a basic necessity, and there were only a few ways of getting them—quilting, knitting or weaving. Women cleaned, carded, spun, and wove wool in their own homes. They cut and pieced old garments into quilt tops by themselves, too. But when it came time to put quilt tops, bottoms, and batting together, they gathered in groups. That they had the opportunity to sit together and could take pleasure from the work was a bonus. If the quilt was attractive that was another plus, but no one could say it wasn't work and it wasn't productive—it was teamwork and recycling at its best.

"Waste not; want not," the women said.

The other time a woman could relax was at church. Ickka and everyone she knew were good Lutherans. Without overstatement, it's possible to say that the church was an absolute necessity in her life and the lives of those around her. It wasn't just their source of spiritual sustenance, it was their best form of routine entertainment, the church their sole exposure to man-made art, the singing their only regular source of music. Children, of course, sang the folk songs passed down through time or the rare popular ditty that filtered out from the cities. Men learned and sang ribald music in their taverns. But for women? Except for a marriage or other festive occasion when someone splurged and hired musicians, the church sang and played for them.

On Sundays, therefore, Ickka would wash her face and hands and put on her best dress—she had several now—don bonnet and shawl, and join the rest of the village walking the mile to church. For the more prosperous men, Sunday was a day of rest as the Bible ordained. For the women, Sunday was a day of extra cooking. But they did have several hours of relaxation in the church.

Ickka, still silently grieving the loss of her baby at the end of her first year of marriage, may well have found comfort in the streams of words, the prayers, the sermons, the reminders that other people had problems and cried in private over their own losses as she did over hers, that they needed praying over as did she. Not that Ickka would admit it. Nor would she be caught whining. Her back never bent but remained ramrod straight. She had her pride.

Thus, the seasons turned and life in Ludwigsdorf continued. In the next seven years, Ickka, would tuck her first son, her lost baby, into a deep corner of her heart and turn her attention to the children that came after.

The first of these was another boy. He was given the same name as his dead brother, Gerd Janssen, being named in the old way. His paternal grandfather's first name became his first name and was followed by the plural form of the father's name.

As for the old man, Gerd Berens Hinrichs Buss? He passed away after seeing this grandson, never knowing he had founded a line of descendants that would, within five generations, number in the thousands. Nor could he have any idea that his name would be on the cover of a twenty-first century book.

Grandfather Gerd was buried, and grandson Gerd thrived. Ickka had her son, someone to love unreservedly, someone to love her at least for the first few years of his life. Soon enough he would be weaned away from her by Jann and the other men. He would be taken to help in the fields and on the boats. He would be sent to the parish church to learn his letters and his numbers. Soon enough, he would come to think about his mother in the way many other men regarded their women, as indentured-for-life servants. But not yet.

Even with a baby at her breast, even though Jann now had a son, this was likely not a happy home. As we'll see by Jann's actions in the coming years, he does not seem to have been a happy man or a loving husband and father. More probably, he ruled his domestic life with an iron fist and an absence of patience. His rule for wife and children, we can assume, was: "When I say jump, you say how high."

Which would not have made for a pleasant environment for Ickka, even with her big house and new baby. In fact, her best days might've been the ones where Jann was gone. Likewise, for Jann, his happiest times might well have been the hours he could forget his domestic situation, times spent on his boat or hobnobbing with his business acquaintances or enjoying the pleasures offered by 'ladies' in the harbor houses.

Next Ickka had a girl child, Elsche Catherina Janssen. The little girl's birth was a mixed blessing. Fortunately, Elsche came after Ickka had produced a healthy boy. An occasional girl was not a bad thing. She could be a comfort to the mother and a help in the home, but she would never be seen as capable of doing the hard work that meant survival for the community, and no one did much rejoicing over the arrival of a girl.

At least, Ickka would know, the girl would be hers for the next fifteen or sixteen years. When Elsche Catherina married, she would leave, would go to live with her in-laws, perhaps never to be seen again. Girl babies like boy babies were loaners, only the length of the loan was different.

The next pregnancy was another girl, one they named Janna Janssen. All of Jann's children would have his name as their middle names, just as he had his father, Gerd's, name as his second name. He was Jann Gerdes. They were Gerd Janssen. Elsche Catharina Janssen, and Janna Janssen. That was custom.

These first years passed swiftly as time does when a person is busy. Everyone, everywhere in Europe wanted Friesen peat for their fires. The Friesens couldn't cut it fast enough to keep up, and Jann and his fellow boatmen were never lacking in cargo. In fact, Jann's canal transport business prospered, and he bought himself another boat.

Things were just as satisfactory for him at home. Despite his likely discontent with the marriage, Ickka had proved an excellent incubator and mother, so much so that he, like the children, took to calling her "Moder" or mother. She was a jewel, as well, at husbanding his resources, never spending a *thaler* more than necessary. Little in her household ever needed replacing, just repairing.

But while she saved, Jann spent, most conspicuously on the new boat. If Ickka dared to voice an opinion, it would've been: "We could have used that money to buy more land." Throughout her life, the purchase of land was her solution to the question of security. Land was the only thing that held its value no matter what. "Land," she would not just teach her children but instill in their very genes, "is the only investment worth making."

Jann wouldn't have argued the point, but he may have unbent enough to explain a basic economic reality. "A larger boat will add to what we can carry and help us meet the people's needs and keep our customers happy. And we will have much more profit." His figures proved it. There was really no argument.

Even so, to be Ostfriesen was to have an atavistic sense about land. "You never go hungry if you own your own land," the old ones said. Land equaled security. More, being country people, they measured a man's worth and his wealth not by cash or possessions but by land.

In this context, Jann's boat purchase had the aura of risky behavior about it. When things went wrong, and they always did sooner or later, you couldn't eat a boat. And, it wouldn't keep you warm unless you burned it, which would make for very expensive heating.

Things Fall Apart

Eighteen hundred and forty-five was the year of Janna's birth. In general, it was a year of content for the Buss family. Except for the likely difference of opinion over the new boat, Jann and Ickka may have grown accustomed to each other and as satisfied as they'd ever be with their union. They each had their own spheres.

The children would have had lives much like Ickka had experienced in the Eilerts' home with the addition of more and more varied foods and a bit more warmth. Otherwise, from the moment she could walk, Elsche Katharina would have had her chores as Ickka had had before her—ones tailored to her ability and designed to teach her the many skills she would need to master in the coming years. Most likely, she also had a doll or two, probably made from dried husks and scraps of cloth. Big brother, Gerhard, was four the year Janna joined them and would already take for granted his daily farm chores. When he had time to play, his games would mostly be anticipatory and involve things like digging and damning little ditches and making stick boats to sail on them. But, like other boys of all ages and cultures, he would also be exploring his environment, finding secret places, and building friendships.

"He will be a farmer, a good farmer," Ickka probably said on more than one occasion as the women compared notes with each other about their offspring. As for Jann, he may have wanted something more for his son. Of course, the boy must know about farms and farming, but he should also learn about boats, canals, and the sea. He might even grow up to own his own merchant ship or—dare one hope—a fleet of them.

But it was 1846. That summer the rains stopped all across Europe. Without them the world everyone knew cracked and began a process of disintegration. By January 1847, Jann's old boat undoubtedly lay idle at its moorings and his new boat had precious little work. This was disturbing but far from catastrophic since Jann still had land, animals, and a house. But his source of cash was ebbing as fast as a moon-driven tide. His cargo-hauling business was at a standstill, his tenants would likely be in arrears on their rents, and where would he get the money to pay his taxes when they came due in on May 1, 1847? But, surely, the drought would ease. Surely, 1847 would be a good year.

It wasn't.

4
Europe 1846-1848

Across the land during those sad excuses for years—1846 and 1847—Catholics, Lutherans, Church of England, ministers, priests, and preachers took as their text Revelation 6:5-6, the part where the New Testament says: "And when he had opened the third seal, I heard the third beast say, 'Come and see.' And I beheld, and lo a black horse; and he that sat on him had a pair of balances in his hand." With rising voice, ministers and priests and pastors thundered to the people: "Thus comes the third horseman of the Apocalypse on his black horse, and his name is famine, and he is God's wrath let loose on a land of sinners."

A Europe which had just begun to recover from the dislocations of the Napoleonic conquests, staggered and was brought to its knees by the dry spring of 1846, one that was followed by hot winds and cracked, dusty fields of July and August. Prayers that 1847 would bring good rains or at least marginal moisture proved futile. Almost everywhere the crops failed. The sun glared. Dust gathered on windowsills and settled like ragged garments on houses in towns as far away as Sicily and as close as Hannover. People were reduced to skeletons, children's bellies swelled with malnutrition, old people went to bed and never woke again. Immigrant ships—soon called coffin ships—sailed to America filled with those trying to escape only to die on the crossing or when they were turned away from the United States or when they reached land in Canada.

As though wide-spread starvation was not enough, the potato blight came in on the heels of the drought. Even when there was rain, potatoes rotted in their fields. A man could look out with pride and hope on strong, green plants in the morning and find wilting tops and blackened roots in the evening. Where this wonderful food had become a staple, more people starved.

Ostfriesens, off in their remote and sea-soaked fens, were spared the initial onslaught of crop failure, water being the curse of this land, not its blessing. Certainly, putting food on the table was not Ickka's problem in 1846 and 1847. Her situation—Jann's situation—was a bit more complicated, largely because he'd entered Europe's emerging middle class thanks to Ostfriesland's peat economy.

Famine in Europe changed that.

Poverty followed farm failures, and the demand for peat dropped. People just couldn't afford to buy at any price, and it wasn't long before the ships that had carried the popular fuel rocked and creaked in their anchorages. Peat cutters found their pockets empty, their source of cash gone and their hands idle. They went back to subsistence living. Those who had a bit of land grew what they needed to survive and relied as they always had on their close-knit family groups as a safety net. People shared. Kin looked after kin.

But even in the best of times there were many who had to seek work in neighboring provinces or migrate to the cities where the industrial revolution had reached and where factories paid low wages for back-breaking labor. Now, even those opportunities—as poor as they had been—no longer existed. A man would need to go much further afield to earn wages, would have to leave Europe altogether.

Ostfriesen emigration to new worlds had started decades

before with a trickle of single men and a few families setting out for Australia, New Zealand, and America. They were forerunners or at least they hoped they were. To that end they wrote long letters home telling of the conditions they found, offering advice, encouraging others to follow. Their adjectives glowed. Their verbs were positive; their nouns florid and their negatives negligible.

In another time and place, the numbers tempted would probably have amounted to no more than a trickle. But in the bad years of 1846 and 1847, the letters had an effect. There was free land to be had. A man could ride his own horse like a lord. Wild game was everywhere and easily hunted. Prairie grasses provided endless and free pasturage for cattle, horses, pigs, sheep, and goats. The new worlds were magical places. All you had to do was get yourself there, which is what numbers of young men began to do. Thus, ships sailing from the port of Bremen filled with cargos of emigrants, and some of those, too, became coffin ships.

Emigration wasn't the only outlet for men and women deprived of hope. Now, the word "revolution" crept into the average vocabulary. Elsewhere in Europe, a new middle class spawned groups of liberals and self-styled socialists who stepped into the power vacuum left by the collapse of the Napoleonic empire, agitating for change. In the process, they promised much to the people. Men like Karl Marx and Frederick Engels, as one example, preached the idea that all men should profit equally from the fruits of labor. In 1848, Marx would publish that Bible of the workers movement: *The Communist Manifesto*. Other political theories proliferated as well and found hopeful ears among the masses of unemployed, hungry, and much-exploited workers.

Mix these voices for change with famine, extreme social and economic inequality, stir well, and … The result? Rioting and civil disobedience plagued towns and cities across Europe. People took to the streets, venting their fears and frustrations. From north to south and east to west uprisings made headlines. News of them spread inspiring yet more riots. Cities and villages alike were subject to tramping feet, hoarse cries, and varying degrees of violence. From France through the Italian and Germanic states, people rioted and revolted, rampaged around their neighborhoods, looted and ravaged their own cities. Thousands died in this way and many more in the retaliations that followed.

Thanks to their isolation, their agrarian economy, and their water, Ostfriesens again had a certain immunity. Yes. Prussia profited from the upheavals by extending the Kaiser's power over Hannover and, thus, over Ostfriesland. But, after all, their little bit of land had been swapped around time after time during the past hundred years, so much so that you almost had to live it to keep track of who was nominally governing and from where. As we've seen, the capitol city might be Berlin, London, Amsterdam, Paris, or Hannover. The leader might be a king, emperor, duke, or elector. So what if in 1846 and 1847, their land was again up for grabs? So what if in 1848 their taxes again went straight to Berlin?

But as I said, it was bad enough. Ships sat idle at their moorings. Sailors and shippers, freight handlers and boatmen, whores and pub owners all scrounged to stay alive. With no money coming in via shipping and peat sales, coin didn't filter into the countryside and in time the village pubs closed, thatchers and builders had no work, and the depression spread. And how would anyone pay their taxes? And what about the homeless and hopeless roaming the countryside and cleaning out gardens and fields in the dark of night? And what could a man do if the taxman seized his little scrap of land for non-payment of taxes?

No. The Ostfriesens didn't revolt. But they weren't happy. There were taxes that had to be paid. There was hunger and something else: conscription.

Ostfriesens had been allowed to pay to keep their young men from being conscripted under Hannoverian rule. The boys didn't have to flee before the conscripting units, not if they could afford to buy their way out. But now? Who had the necessary money to buy a boy's way out of military service, to keep him from becoming canon fodder, to preserve a beloved son's bones from the fate of moldering in some foreign grave.

And it wasn't as though a young man could pass unnoticed. Not with troops billeted in every neighborhood—living in the roomier houses, displacing livestock from their biers, eating food needed for children. At least, these troops were only there to prevent trouble. They weren't hunting rebels through Ostfriesen villages as they were in surrounding provinces where riots had taken place and where the ruling classes were fighting back. Elsewhere, soldiers were shooting suspects, raping women, and setting fire to houses and fields. But not in Ostfriesland. Or not much.

Thus, in the truly terrible year of 1847, Ostfriesland was, in a way, blessed.

Yes. But life, always hard, had become harder. In the meantime, Ostfriesens went about their business, took care of each other as best they could or as their dispositions allowed, hiked their belts in another notch, and watched the more adventurous or desperate among them emigrate. In church on Sundays they prayed for peace, for good harvests, for economic and political stability, and a return of the peat trade. And they thanked their Lutheran God that the worst of the devastations had passed them by.

5
Big Decisions

Sitting around a peat fire of an evening, Jann and his friends read aloud, spelling out words sent from America that spoke about a great land bursting with opportunity, a continent where every man was his own king, a virgin country where men and even women could spread their arms wide and own everything to the horizon. Ickka, with her mending or darning, her spinning or weaving, would have listened to all of this and been silent.

"As far as the eye can see," Jann read, "this land is covered with grass so high it hides the animals in their thousands who feed on it. And it is all either free or to be had for low cost, ready to bear crops, needing only to be planted and harvested. No one goes hungry. We eat meat and drink milk every day. The rivers are full of fish, the prairie thick with deer and bison and elk, the skies dark with geese and ducks. The name of this land is Texas."

No one goes hungry.

Ickka was not a woman to throw the idleness of Jann's boats up in his face. Nor would Jann have tolerated the reminder. Still, both realized the cold hard truth: if he'd saved his money, America wouldn't be looking so good.

Night after night, week after week during the winter of 1846-1847 Jann must have brooded about his options while Ickka probably brought home news related by the other women about America. "The price of a cow in America is just $4," she might say. "This is what they say. They say a man can soon have an entire dairy herd."

Jann must have heard much the same but in more detail as he met with the other men, all of them debating the possibilities. Gradually as February advanced into March with no sign of the usual winter and early spring rains, the idea of America began to seem less a dream and more like a real possibility. Jann was in his prime. His wife was just twenty-five; he thirty-five. They would have to sell everything here to have enough money for the transatlantic fare and to purchase land, animals, and tools in America. They would have to sell everything he'd worked all of his life to accumulate, but it was vanishing, anyway. Here was an opportunity to escape his own failures. Best of all, he wouldn't seem to be running away. He'd be running toward a brilliant future.

But even considering all the positives, could he abandon the house his parents had built, leave all of his relatives and friends, jump to a place where he didn't speak the language or know the customs, turn his back on the big safety net made by the tight-knit familial relationships?

On the positive side, he wouldn't be alone. Other Ostfriesens had already set up communities in Texas and up the Mississippi. Their letters told him everything he needed to know to make a successful beginning, starting with advice on what to take and even including where to find help along the way. Language would be a problem, of course, but he had a nodding acquaintance with English from dealing with the English shippers and because Plattdeutsch incorporated hundreds of English words, just pronounced them differently. Besides, the letters said there were agents along the way who specialized in translating for immigrants. So how hard could it be?

Then there was the matter of his dependents. They were all toddlers—little Janna just two years old. How safe was it undertake the hazardous journey to America and into a wilderness with them? He had to have heard of the coffin ships, of the death rate among those crammed into steerage. He knew, too, of the many ways women and children died on the American prairies.

Gerd Franken, his brother-in-law, became another factor in Jann's deliberations. Gerd, his sister Gesche's husband, seems never to have done particularly well for himself. By the winter of 1846-47, his mother had passed away, reducing his number of dependents, and his boys were eleven and eight, both old enough and big enough to help out. If only there was work to be had. Now, 1 May 1847 loomed on Gerd's calendar as a disaster waiting to happen. For on May Day both his contractual tenant obligations and the annual taxes on his house would come due.

Emigration would seem an ideal solution to Gerd. The catch was, still, money. Ship owners and captains required payment of passage in advance and absolutely refused to allow a man to work his way across the Atlantic. It was cash on the barrelhead or no ticket to America. To get around this, many men and women indentured themselves to others for specific periods of time.

Gerd could do this. Sale of his dower house would bring some money, maybe enough for the fares … if he could find a buyer. For the rest, he could, in a sense, indenture himself and his boys.

"We could all go together," Gerd may well have proposed to Jann. "This is the perfect time to leave, coming after the big winter storms and getting us to America in time to plant for this summer. With your money and our labor we could accomplish much." Besides, it was also customary for family to work with family. They were a team. They were a unit.

Or, it might not have been that way at all.

Whatever, Gerd did dispose of all of his possessions. He did land in America with only a few dollars in his pocket.

Now comes an interesting twist in the story. Gerd changed his name and the names of his wife and children long enough to board ship. Why? How did he get away with it?

The 'how' part is easy. Hannoverian authorities were not very strict about emigration in 1846 when Jann and Gerd must have begun considering the subject. That would change after the summer of 1848 as the numbers of citizens wanting to leave swelled into the tens of thousands. But in 1846 and 1847, all a man needed was to present proof of identity. In this period of still flexible identities, that posed no problem.

As I've mentioned, surnames were still a recent phenomenon, while the other trappings of a modern society—birth certificates, drivers licenses, passports, and identity cards—had yet to be invented or become common. How to establish identity then? Most Ostfriesens could point to their name inscribed in a church register. If they owned land, they had their name on a tax roll.

And, that's the how. But why?

Another element of the law seems to have been the problem. A potential emigrant had to show he had no outstanding debts or a criminal record or had failed in any way to be a law-abiding citizen. Apparently, Gerd Tjark Franken could not do this. But was it debts or a criminal record or something else?

We know he was poor, so possibly his problem was something as minor as back taxes on his cottage. Perhaps he had defaulted on tenant payments. Maybe it was a youthful indiscretion. It's unlikely to have been a criminal matter. Certainly, such a taint would've crept into family histories. Or one would think so.

Whatever it was, Gerd Franken did not try to emigrate. Tjark Berend and family boarded ship; then disappeared, lost somewhere on the Atlantic Ocean. The family Franken arrived in the port of New Orleans. Neither Gerd nor any other family member would use the Berend name again. In short, Tjark Berend and family would appear briefly on the stage, long enough to get past the authorities and sail from Bremerhaven, then vanish.

The Sale, 1847

On Thursday, April 15, 1847, Jann went into the nearest large town, Aurich, to place an advertisement in the *Amtsblatt fur die Provinz Ostfriesland*. He'd made up his mind in favor of emigration, had much to sell, and would need to attract buyers from afar as it was unlikely that people in the surrounding villages had money to spare. Thus, on April 21st, the auctioneer arrived, the buyers gathered, and the big sale began in the village's largest venue—the inn owned by Heye Mimken Flessner.

Ickka would have spent the month preceding the auction rushing from job to job. She had her normal work to do, had three toddlers to tend, and now needed to sort out what would be given to relatives, what would be sold, and what to take to America. The latter? Precious little, because Jann had decided to sail steerage. He could afford better, but they would not travel in one of the new and fairly comfortable steam ships, nor even in one of the larger sailing ships with passenger accommodations.

No. Jann was not spending one thaler more than absolutely necessary on fares. They would travel in the cheapest possible way—in steerage on a small barque. While the ship he selected did not have a history as a coffin ship, it was exactly the sort to become one, differing from them only in the matter of captain and crew and their port of departure.

Presumably, Jann thought this through, deciding that the

loss of one or more children or a wife was an acceptable price to pay. Because the odds were high that would happen. But to be fair to Jann, he was risking his life, as well.

Despite the economic downturn and the uncertainties of the time, the auction would have drawn a good crowd. Everyone who could do so always turned out for an auction. It was a time to visit with friends and neighbors, to meet with those from nearby villages, and to tell jokes and hear gossip. Most of all, though, men attended to take the economic pulse of the district and to get an idea of where values stood. How much would a cow bring? What about a bred cow? How much for a yoke of oxen or a clock or a quilt? Were people starting to feel optimistic? Were people who still had money willing to spend it?

No one had much hope of brisk bidding. The signs for a good agricultural year were poor as, across most of Europe, the spring rains had completely failed to materialize. Those who knew these things (and those who didn't) were saying 1847's drought would be worse than that of 1846, and everyone expected the potato blight to strike again in Ireland and other potato-growing regions.

The women of the village probably appeared at Ickka's door to offer their sympathy for her situation, sitting to share a cup of tea, a drink that the Ostfriesens had adopted as their own. Noses inhaling the rich aroma of the steaming brew, the same women who had extolled the positives would now give vent to their fears.

"They say those savage red men in America rape the women they capture, then burn them."

"Yes, and they say you can travel for days and never see another person."

"Have you heard? The winters are so bad the snow buries the

houses and the people suffocate."

"But, really, it is the crossing that is the worst. Great storms break up the ships, hundreds of them go down every year and all aboard drown."

"Humph. Isn't it always this way. The men go for adventure. They take their guns and disappear to enjoy shooting, but they leave the women alone with the children to find their own food and survive as best they can. If they can."

"And the diseases. There is this flux, as they call it, which kills within hours. A daughter is well in the morning and playing but by noon she is dead, the mother by evening." The dire warnings were endless; voiced in syrupy tones.

As for Ickka, she was most likely conflicted. On the one hand, change could be exciting and she was still young enough to think so. This would be a grand adventure with the possibility of a huge payout in the coin she most craved—land. Also, she was hugely practical, and she could read the tea leaves as well as Jann could. The wonderful days of Ostfriesen prosperity were over for the foreseeable future, a future in which they might well see their holdings melt away. The very thought of being cold and hungry again, certainly, would have been enough to make Ickka sign on.

On the other hand, she would be leaving a home she'd come to love, would be taking her children into danger, and—this was the worst of all bad timings—her menses had stopped. She was pregnant again.

No matter the potential hardships and second thoughts, the Buss and Franken families were committed, were preparing to emigrate to America. It seems probable that the day Jann placed his auction advertisement he expected to book passage almost immediately after the sale, to arrive at his destination in May 1847.

It didn't work that way. The auction did not produce an immediate sale of Jann's properties. Instead, he signed a contract which had as stipulations that the buyer would make his last payment and take possession in March 1848.

For Ickka this would have come as a reprieve. She would bear the child now beginning to swell her belly in her own bed. Surely, this would be better than trying to deliver a baby in the wilderness of America under totally unknown conditions.

In the event, Heinrich Janssen was born in December of 1847. Three months later, the Buss and Franken families left their homes in Ludwigsdorf, never to see them again. Jann and Gerd were carrying their wives and seven children into both known and unknown danger.

Departure

Jann found berths for all of them on the English sailing ship, *Elizabeth*, out of Bremerhaven, bound for New Orleans, due to depart on 15 March 1848. To reach it on time, they left Ludwigsdorf well before that date. While only a trip of some fifty miles with the first leg of it by canal boat, the roads from there on to Bremerhaven would be difficult. It was best to give themselves plenty of time. More, they were not traveling light and had to deal with seven children—Gesche and Gerd Franken's two boys, age 12 and 9 now, and their girl, age 6 and the Buss children, ages 6, 5, 3 and 3 months.

The children were serious, of course, but excited, the baby traveling in a sling carried by Ickka. The boys wanted to be of help, but the trunks weighed approximately 100 pounds each—the maximum allowed—and were much too large for them to heft. The smaller boxes and bundles, one for each person, were another matter. These contained what the two families would need for the one to two months of their sea voyage. The trunks would go in the hold below the passenger deck, the boxes containing utensils, food, and fuel would stay with them and double as seats in their allotted space.

ELIZABETH · 1846

Every passenger on the *Elizabeth* had been required to bring aboard sufficient food for ten weeks. The recommended foodstuffs for an Atlantic crossing were: bacon, ham, dried meat, flour, peas, Capuchin peas, bread (cut and dried), toast, vinegar, salt, mustard, pepper, coffee, tea. They would also have herbal remedies, a teakettle, one cast iron pot, tin bowls, tin plates, water jugs, a bucket plus a selection of beverages such as wine, brandy, rheinwein, soured milk, and juniper schnapps. The ship's master would have put in a supply of lemons or limes, as well. The citrus might be necessary if scurvy became a problem.

Once in America, Jann had been assured, he could buy almost everything they might need for good prices. Ten dollars would purchase a cow and calf; $15 a horse. Bricks came at 20 cents/bushel, meat at 2 cents/pound, bacon for 2+ cents/pound. In short, the Buss family would be able to afford to buy grade foundation stock and enough food to get them through until the first harvest/butchering.

Tuesday, 14 March 1848. The great exodus that was to come had yet to mobilize the government in Hannover. The big emigration facility that would process most of the 7 million souls who would depart for the New World did not yet exist, and the departure formalities were minimal—formalities Jann had already handled. He had their exit papers in his pocket, and they could proceed directly to the wharf where the *Elizabeth* waited.

Once they were aboard, there wasn't much to see. The *Elizabeth* was a small sailing ship built for the transatlantic trade, her hull sheathed for protection in warm waters. On this voyage her cargo would be human, but no one had bothered to convert her into anything approximating a passenger ship. There were no cabins, no heads, no dining rooms, no partitions. There were no cooks, no cleaners, and no law except what the captain or the passengers, themselves, imposed.

The *Elizabeth* was one step up from a slaver, the major differences being the lack of chains and the slightly larger space allowance per person on wooden platforms built as bunks. That said, like a slaver, a certain percentage of its human cargo was expected to die. Like a slaver, when the trip was complete, presuming the *Elizabeth* survived the trip, her hold would have to be stripped, fumigated, and washed with ammonia and lye.

At least, because of the horrors of the previous sailing season, there were now laws about how many bodies a ship could carry—the figure based on the ship's cargo space. The *Elizabeth* would sail with her maximum of 192 passengers. Of these, only 29 were under the age of 15. The four infants aboard were not counted. The Franken/Buss party, thus, was not exactly the average, having one of the infants and six of the children aboard (20% of the total number). The Franken/Buss family would also be singled out for another statistic—Gerd at 47 was almost the oldest passenger. None of this promised well for the family's survivability.

Which brings us to Gerd. In this period, a man could expect to live to age 50. Gerd, thus, was incredibly old to be undertaking such a journey. The fact that he had to adopt an alias? The additional fact that upon arrival he had an empty pocket? Encumbered by a wife and three children and with no financial resources, Gerd launched himself on a journey many young, single men would not consider. All of this speaks, at a minimum, to desperation and determination (if not to courage and bravery) and a steely resolve to break with the past and give his boys a better future. If they survived. Gerd, like Jann, knew the stories.

The big difference between Gerd and Jann? Gerd could not afford more, and his financial situation in Ludwigsdorf had become critical. Gerd made the same decision that tens of thousands of others would make out of the same need. You can see love and responsibility as well as dire necessity in the choice. For Jann? Even if he did purchase tickets for the Frankens, it was all optional.

Thus, for their various reasons, they took their lives in their hands and boarded the *Elizabeth*. In that moment they all saw for the first time just how small and fragile and cramped the ship was--not much larger than Ickka's cow byre. And her cow byre with its brick walls was much, much more durable. What would happen here with weeks of no wind or days of seas that towered higher than the highest buildings in Bremerhaven?

"Dear God in Heaven."

Their new world had masts ringed in iron that rose fore and aft like solid trees, their roots planted below the deck. They saw the big wheel that steered the vessel and two deck cabins of about twelve-by-fifteen feet—more like shacks—one forward and one astern.

As Ickka climbed the plank and rope gangway, her two little girls clinging to her skirts, the baby in a sling, and her arms filled with bundles, she probably noticed a big square hole forward which seemed to be the access point to the hold because a rope winch was moving netted trunks and crates from the wharf to the ship and lowering them into the darkness. Piles of hemp cables lay here and there, while only a low, curving railing circled the deck, one that would do little to stop a body from falling right off the deck and into the sea.

"Dear God in Heaven."

There was nothing else to be said. Steep steps, more ladder than stairs, led down through a second hole to what they called the "In Between Decks" and we know as the 'Tween Decks. When Ickka climbed down, she saw six to eight weeks into her future—a very grim future indeed.

There, in near darkness, lined up on both sides of the ship, head to toe, were double-decked platforms of rough-cut wood, each pair about ten-feet wide by six-feet long, each holding a flat mattress of ticking, presumably filled with straw, each labeled with a number. The lower sleeping platform sat about a foot off the deck, the upper platform was less than three feet above that. There wasn't even enough room between for an adult to sit up. The center of the deck nearest the hatch where Ickka entered would already have been piled with boxes and bags. A few lanterns provided small pools of illumination showing women and men spreading blankets, claiming a small piece of space as their own. Each platform was meant to sleep five people.

Impossible to know Ickka's thoughts as she got her first look at the press of strangers who seemed to swim before her as disembodied pale blobs for faces as she listened to the clamor of women arguing over space and children crying, men yelling, of pushing and shoving, of the rolling thunder of many heavily booted feet tramping on hollow decking.

Even in this first glimpse of her new world, Ickka probably would have noticed one more negative—the tall Ostfriesens didn't fit. Most of the men and many of the women were stooped, their heads jutting forward to avoid the beams. With clearance of only 5' under the beams and not much more from floor to ceiling, their bodies scrunched down, adding to the discomfort.

And, the smell. There was the strong odor of wet wool and wet linen, of course. But the other thing? It wasn't strong, was more like the memory of a smell, a lingering miasma that clung to the ship's timbers despite the stronger odors of tar and fresh-cut wood, of hemp and lamp oil. The smell was well-known to everyone in Ostfriesland, because it hovered over every cesspit behind every house in the province, and it would have been one more reminder—sickness and death haunted voyages to America.

Then there were the people ... strangers. Had Ickka ever seen so many strangers in such close proximity in her entire life? Probably not. Her world had been limited to a closed circle of friends who were probably distant relatives and cousins, aunts, and uncles whose consanguinity was known without reference to the church records. Now, here were these people with unfamiliar features, some of whom didn't even speak her language.

For better or worse, they would be her close companions in the coming weeks. She would come to know them more intimately than she knew any but members of her immediate family. How well she got on with them would make a big difference in the quality of her and her children's lives, might even be important to their survival. It's just as well she had no idea of the many ways a child could die in a sea crossing aboard a ship like this. But she would learn.

6
The Crossing

In the wee hours of the morning of the 15th of March, Captain P. Barclay gave the order, men scrambled into the riggings, loosed sail, and with hatches open the ship moved out on the tide, finding her way into the North Sea where she turned west before catching a fair wind and running south down the English Channel. Days later she rounded Ireland to face the Atlantic. Waves slapped the ship's sides, lifted her high, or sent her down into deep troughs. Her prow cut through the waters. Sick or well, young or old, male or female, there was no turning back.

Ahead of them? Who knew. But if everything went right, if the weather was with them, if they had luck on their side, the *Elizabeth* could make New Orleans in six weeks, running down the English Channel, hitting the westerly-blowing trade winds off the coast of Great Britain, scudding before the wind, all sails set, across the Atlantic and into the Caribbean where she would turn north, round Florida, and beat her way up to her destination.

That's if everything went well. On the other hand, contrary winds had kept many a ship from even sailing south through the English Channel. Some ships spent weeks just trying to get out of the North Sea. Once in the Atlantic, a spring storm could blow them far off course, generally south toward the equator where their ship might be stuck for weeks at a time before, eventually and with food and drink supplies diminished to the vanishing point, clawing their way into the Gulf of Mexico.

A degree of starvation was far from uncommon aboard the immigrant ships when the expected crossing lengthened and lengthened again. Death from starvation, however, was rare, primarily because the weakened body became vulnerable to disease or careless in high seas, and these forms of mortality easily took the famished. Once it became clear to a family that their food supply would not last, though, they might have the opportunity to purchase more from a passing vessel. In those cases, the cost was excessive. But, if the family had the money, they could avoid that particular hazard.

There were few rules aboard ship. Neither the captain nor the crew was particularly interested in what happened in the hold. Nor did they mind passengers spending as much time as they wanted on deck as long as they kept out of the way of the sailors. As someone was bound to have said, "What do they care if you get washed overboard or if the 'tween decks fills up with dead bodies? They already have your money."

Except the authorities didn't have all their money, and what the passengers carried aboard was a matter of interest to some. Before departure, the Hannoverian government had required every emigrant to sell all of his possessions (except what he was allowed to take with him). Thus, emigrants traveled with their worldly goods transformed into gold and sewn into their clothing or tucked into money belts. On the *Elizabeth?* Probably the amounts were small—Gerd Franken, for example, had only two pistoles to his name. Jann, on the other hand, would have been among the richest aboard the *Elizabeth* with an even 100.

One hundred pieces of real gold could be enough to make a poor man salivate and tempt the less honest among the mostly single male passengers. It could be so easy to slip a hand into a money belt in the crammed 'tween deck, so easy to steal. And it wasn't just gold. Even food supplies—especially food supplies—were a potential target and vulnerable.

Jann, from his experience around the docks, was aware of these hazards. He knew the critical importance of establishing a firm self-governing and self-enforcing body to keep order among the passengers, to suppress whatever criminal element might be aboard. Thus, it's likely he jockeyed with a handful of other men in the serious business of organizing a leaderless group to deal with their mutual need for security. He knew that the effectiveness of their deliberations would determine the kind of life they had 'tween decks and how many survived the crossing.

The low death rate on this transit indicates that these passengers took their organizing seriously.

The women, like the stalwart Ickka, no doubt tried to make things as comfortable as possible, to create some sort of a routine and an environment that would keep their families healthy during the passage ahead. They worried about dry clothing, about food preparation, about ways to treat a long list of ailments from chilblains to broken bones, from scurvy to seasickness. There was no ship's medical kit, no doctor, no reference material—just the women and their home-taught skills.

The women would also have pushed their husbands to rig canvas during rain storms in order to collect water for washing and to organize them to scrape down the vomit and waste-spewed flooring regularly with sea water and ammonia as well as to enforce sanitary codes. In the days to come, they would bless and curse the hatches which let light and air into the 'tween deck but leaked water during storms. At least there was a stove which meant easier drying for clothes that seemed to be wet all of the time during those first weeks.

On the 'tween deck, life moved to the pitch and yaw of the hull, some of the passengers adapting and developing an insensitivity to the rancid smells of close-packed humanity. Others were seasick from the moment they left Bremerhaven, the contents of their stomachs fouling straw ticks, platforms, and floor. Their bladders and bowels, of course, gave way as well, adding to the miasma and filth. A person could become sick just from living in proximity to such foul sights and smells … and did.

The Hell of It All

At sea you could die in any number of ways, of course, but only the doomsayers among the passengers wanted to enumerate them. The reality of loss was enough. On the *Elizabeth*, four men were washed overboard, one a boy of only fourteen. Four was actually a very good record. Also, no one died of disease. These facts spoke well of the ship's captain, P. Barkley, and of the passengers' concern for safety and attest to their creating and following rules for cleanliness.

Even so and even with constant cleaning and periodic fumigating using steam from chlorine, the stench 'tween decks would have been overwhelming. Mostly, though, the passengers stayed out of the 'tween deck as much as possible and kept their spirits up by dancing on the main deck in the cool of a calm evening, by putting on clean clothes at least once a week, by participating in endless games, and by enjoying performances by people who'd brought musical instruments. Captain Barclay read the services on Sundays, and everyone attended—some from religious conviction and need, some because of the entertainment value.

The children made their own games, just as they had at home, using whatever came to hand as props or toys. The ship's rats, for example, would have been popular. The older boys made slingshots and went hunting in the hold. The younger ones, like Gerd, probably captured rat babies and turned them into pets before accident or their own mothers put an end to that. There was little that could rouse a scream from a mother faster than the site of a rodent's head protruding from under a boy's collar or sticking out of his pocket.

The women had little patience for such antics and few had an excess of time. They had children to watch and see to, food to be prepared, bedding to be hauled on deck to air, and endless doctoring of and cleaning up after the sick. They had fires to make and dirty diapers to wash and try to dry. When these things were done, there were socks to mend, clothing to patch, and garments to be knitted or crocheted.

That said, days went by during which they could do nothing but crouch in their various places holding on as best they could as the ship pitched and rolled. They stopped hearing the wind howling in the rigging above them or the smash and crash of waves breaking over the rails. They closed their eyes against the dark of the hold on these days when no fire or light of any kind was allowed and the hatches were kept closed. No night could be as dark as the 'tween deck during a storm. When they had to move, they groped their way from handhold to handhold, more often than not a seeking hand closing on another passenger.

Even the best disciplined of children became quarrelsome and fussy; babies screamed; fights broke out; women burst into tears; the sick retched and moaned. Everyone, even the strongest and healthiest, suffered.

Food preparation was the big challenge, one handled by women when the sea was calm but given to the men when the weather turned rough. Meals were reduced to the simplest form possible—one pot dishes. The routine was invariable. Gesche and Ickka would be up before the others, as they would at home, first tending to their own ablutions. Warned about the lack of sanitary facilities, Ickka had brought a covered chamber pot with a handle. She and Gesche would be the first to use it in the morning, one holding a blanket as a screen for the other. In a pitching sea, though, this could be a challenge.

Ickka probably wished she'd thought to bring several more covered pots for sea water and rain water, but once the first beer cask had been emptied, it served for seawater from which Ickka could dip a cupful into a basin for washing. The salt left her skin sticky and rough, but better that than filthy. She undoubtedly had rashes and chilblains—everyone did. When she finished, if it was a relatively calm day, the designated keeper of the fire (the job rotated among the passengers) would have built the fire in their pot-bellied stove, and their part of the 'tween deck would warm slightly, motivating the others to roll out of their blankets.

By this time, one of the women would've opened the bread tin and gotten out the box of cups. As her family came, she doled out drinks and a single piece of toasted buckwheat bread to each person, the size of the person determining the size of the bread piece. In good weather they would take their meal up on deck to eat.

In the meantime one of the women or girls would be tending to the peas or the ubiquitous buckwheat groats that had been soaking in beer all night, adding a piece of salted and smoked pork and, perhaps, an onion. With the help of one of the older boys, she would carry the pot and her tripod up on deck, another child trailing with a handful of wood.

The galley consisted of a shack on deck with a plank roof and a smoke hole. A box of sand of about 4'x4'x4', sat in the center of the shack. If the designated family cook was lucky, the hour still being early and many of the passengers yet to rise at all, she would find a place at the fire table, set up her tripod, build a fire, and begin cooking the day's meal. The idea was not to create a hot pot meal by simmering the peas all day, that was not allowed, but simply to heat the pot's ingredients enough to finish softening the peas and warm the meat.

With five or six fires going, smoke became a huge hazard, and periodically during the cooking process the designated chef would leave her pot and go outside to cleanse her lungs of smoke and let tears wash her burning eyes. This was one of the main reasons Gesche and Ickka rotated their cooking chores, and both of them knew how fortunate they were to be able to do so. Not only could they spell each other, but the size of their family meant there was always someone to hold a place in line or guard a pot, carry something, or run for a forgotten item.

Of course, all of this was in context of constant motion and constant risk. If it wasn't a simple matter of negotiating the center aisle 'tween decks without having a keg or crate come loose and slam into a child or a leg with serious consequences, it was dealing with people whose nerves were balanced on a knife edge. Even the most mundane moment could explode unexpectedly. Danger sailed with them just a heartbeat away.

But there were good moments. On a nice day the women would take their meals on deck, sitting in the shade of a sail or mast. They would watch a school of porpoises or a pod of whales, would count the number of flying fish that appeared, or, as they neared land, remark on the sea birds. The boys would throw a line and a hook over the side in the hopes of catching something. The women would stay on deck with their mending and talk about what they might find in America or whether young cousins had married and whether there would be letters from home waiting for them in New Orleans. Some days there would be other ships in view. On at least one occasion a steam vessel probably overtook and passed them, its funnels belching clouds of smoke.

They made friends aboard, as well, and took pleasure in their company.

Ickka worked. She was listed on the ship's passenger list as a laborer—the only woman with a designation in the 'employment' column. She definitely was a worker, perhaps something of a busy body, and everyone called her mother just as her Illinois neighbors soon would.

"Here is Moder," her fellow passengers would say.

There couldn't have been enough hours in the day for her. Ickka along with the other able-bodied women took on the task of cleaning the sick, helping those with no one else to assist them. The single men, in particular, were at the bottom of the pecking order and vulnerable, even the strongest among them brought down by seasickness, reduced to skin and bones, lying in fouled bedding.

Most if not all nights Ickka would have gone to bed with her eyes burning, her body stinking of smoke, her throat raspy, with hands singed by fire and weeping from sores. Her body would have ached with fatigue, her skin bruised from falls and chafed by salt and filth. But still she no doubt gave her family an occasional hot meal and kept as safe an environment as possible for them, and she would listen to the men talk of the promised lands of America where the streets might not be paved with gold and wealth might not wait for them.

But the promise of land? Would they have land? With enough land they would be safe. Land was all they needed.

7
New Orleans, 1848

None too soon the *Elizabeth* reached the Gulf of Mexico and began the slow slog to New Orleans. By then, the immigrants were running out of food and drink. There had been no rain. Thus, there was no drinking water. Instead, there was the sun. None of the Germans aboard had ever known a sun that burned any bit of exposed skin mercilessly, that turned the practical woolens of northern Europe into potato jackets, trapping heat, chafing sweaty skin, and creating fistulous rashes. To add to the general misery, scurvy had made its almost inevitable appearance. Teeth became loose in jaws, skin took on a yellow appearance, and Captain Barclay broke out barrels of citrus, requiring everyone to consume the fruit which had both dried and become moldy during the passage.

It was May, and it was an education. You could die from heat exhaustion in May. Now they understood all too well why letters from earlier immigrants suggested avoiding, except in the winter, the port of New Orleans and the easy water route into the American mid-west. "Better to go to New York and travel overland if you come later than March," the letters said.

"How bad can it be?" Jann had said back in Ludwigsdorf. "And, besides, we are to join the Saathoff group in Texas, and this is the only way to Texas. We must go to New Orleans first, then find a ship to take us along the coast of what they call the Gulf of Mexico."

Many of the fair-skinned passengers suffered terribly, fooled by the effects of the sun reflecting off water and sails, burning them even as they sat in the shade. But wasn't it worse down in the heat and stench of the 'tween deck?

Sixty-two days after leaving Bremerhaven, it all ended. The tug finished towing the *Elizabeth* upstream, and they docked in New Orleans. It was an average crossing in terms of time and better than most in terms of lives lost. Only four dead. Not bad. In fact, extremely good.

As they finished threading through the heavy river traffic and drew up alongside a wharf fronting the third largest city in America, the passengers moved about with a lightness of step unseen in two months. But even before they disembarked, there were hints that this particular piece of the promised land would prove disillusioning.

The first harbingers had arrived as they penetrated the delta—bugs. Clouds of flies of multiple types swarmed down the hatches, attracted by the smell. They were followed by mosquitoes and mites, tiny little bugs no larger than a speck that formed clouds above their heads, and got into their mouths and ears. Despite the heat, the women draped bits of cloth over the babies and infants and wished for hats with veils.

Surely the insect life would not be this bad once they disembarked.

It was worse. The bugs followed them into the noise and confusion of a wealthy port and a growing city, one long notorious for open sewers and heat and disease.

This though was the promised land, the new land, and it was certainly new to them. Never before and never again would Ickka see anything like it. New Orleans boasted the biggest and best of everything. Even then it was known for its crime rate and corrupt police. Even then it had great food and famous restaurants—the world-class Antoine's had opened a few years earlier. Such establishments were bested only by notorious gambling cellars, whorehouses, and dives that put to shame those of other port cities—Hamburg, for example.

Pickpockets, fur traders, minstrels, slaves, and lords filled the markets. One of the most famous of the latter, Prince Achille Murat, had found refuge in New Orleans after the Napoleonic wars and died only the year before. Houses with soaring pillars and elegant balconies elbowed against shanties and brick factories. Natural gas lines had been run through the city bringing gas lights to homes, stores, and streets. Imagine the first sight ever of a city illuminated at night by more than candles, especially to eyes like Ickka's. Except for her brief experience in Bremerhaven en route to the docks, she had only heard talk about cities and never seen gas lights.

Talk and Bremerhaven were inadequate preparation. There was no comparison. Bremerhaven might have lacked the size or the gas lights of New Orleans, but it had faced the world with order and equanimity. Here there was chaos. Finely matched hackneys jostled for space with heavy teams pulling freight wagons, with boys pushing hand carts, with men bent under bales of cotton. Everyone shoved and shouted. Coffles of naked Africans, white women in bonnets, men wearing buckskins and carrying rifles mingled with uniformed soldiers and gamblers, and Ickka may even have seen a little yellow man with slanted eyes and a queue of hair so long it reached his waist. "Chinaman," someone may have explained or may have used the equally popular name for Orientals: "Nipponese."

What could those be?

The river itself was a marvel, home to a dazzling display of craft—riverboats, stream-driven barges and yawls, deep sea sailing ships, scows, ferries, paddle-wheelers, and myriad varieties of small craft.

The sounds made by machines, animals, and men were deafening and incomprehensible. New Orleans was polyglot with French being the dominant language of the time, but in such an international city, most people spoke two or three languages. There were German immigrants among them, and agents fluent in both Platt and Hoch Deutsch waiting to meet ships carrying Germanic immigrants, charging only $3 to interpret a transaction. They bustled about, making more money in a day than many of the immigrants had seen in a year of work.

Then there were the slaves. Possibly Ickka knew slavery existed, but she would never have dreamed of actually seeing a slave and a slave owner or a man being sold on the block or shackled and led in chains through the streets. And, not just the strange-looking black people, either. There were bound white men, women, and children. "Indentured," she was told. "There's a brisk market in indentured servants." There, but for the grace of God and Jann's gold, might have been her in-laws, the Frankens.

How could you tell the difference between the white indentured and the black slaves? They were both bought and sold. Slaves could buy their own freedom; the indentured had to work their way out of their indentures. Both were at the mercy of their masters. Both showed how low any person could inadvertently fall through accident, birth, misadventure, or plain bad luck. New Orleans provided a learning curve for them all, disturbing, and unwelcome.

The Ostfriesen children gawked; the women turned their heads away and prayed.

"Dear God in Heaven."

So many people, so much heat and poor sanitation. Yellow

fever and cholera were the two main killers in the city, periodic epidemics reducing the population. New Orleans was an exciting city, a challenging city, and a deadly one. In fact in less than twelve months the most devastating cholera epidemic in history would hit New Orleans and follow the Buss/Franken families up the Mississippi.

But it was still 1848, and Jann and Gerd had to find passage to Port Lavaca, Texas, first changing their pistoles to dollars at $3.90 each. From Port Lavaca they would travel overland through San Antonio to a nearby town called New Fountain. There they intended to join the Saathoffsche Kolonie, a settlement begun by an acquaintance from Aurich, Mimke Mimkin Saathoff. Letters from Mimke and other Ostfriesens who had started the colony in 1846 had persuaded Jann and Gerd that the cheap and plentiful Texas land was exactly what they wanted.

"The trip from Port Lavaca is arduous," Mimke had written. "We were among the first to come and were not aware of the hazards. Some of our party died because of poisonous snakes, wagon accidents, and disease, and once we reached here we had difficulty adapting to the type of farming and crops that meet success here. But we had help from friendly Indians and from Texas Rangers who lived with us and taught us the ways of this America frontier. Now, if you take the advice we send and are prepared for the journey, you should have no difficulty. More, we will be here to help you in your first years."

There were other Ostfriesens from the *Elizabeth* in their boarding house near the waterfront, and the talk over dinner about the best places in America to settle was brisk. Here the Buss and Franken families finally heard the whole story of the Saathoff experience, about how the Saathoff party had an exceptionally long and arduous crossing, how they'd been blown off course and landed in Galveston. Many were sick, and all of them were half starved, had little money, and no facility with English or Spanish. They wished only to find land. In short, they were easy marks for men they learned were called *empressarios*, men paid to find colonists and sell them land.

Beguiled by the local con men, the immigrants set off on a long and arduous trek across Texas.

We can picture Gesche and Ickka sitting quietly, listening, but probably thinking this Texas would not be a good place to live and raise their children. As the men talked, Ickka would have nursed Heinrich and kept him as protected from bugs as possible with a bit of muslin. Her main concern in New Orleans, though, would have been Janna. The three-year-old had developed a fever.

"Swamp fever," the people in the boarding house most likely said. And, "cool her as you can during the fever and wrap her warmly with the chills." Ickka followed this advice. She'd also bought something called Jesuit bark, which she made into a bitter tea. "If anything will cure her, that is it," some said.

As for their plans to go to Texas, they found they'd have not just another sea voyage but a long trek over land. The latter had been the death of many in the Saathoff group. "Before they reached the town called San Antonio," they heard, "many more of their party died. Mimke tells a true tale about this. Also, in the beginning, as Mimke says, there were Indians who were friendly. Even then, though, these same Indians would steal from them. They would take anything they could, just walking into a house, picking up a gun or a kettle or a coat, and leaving with it."

But that was the good part because now, they were told, those same tribes had turned hostile, realizing the colonists were closing their hunting lands to them. So, a war of small skirmishes had begun. Farmers carried guns into the fields; women and children stayed inside their fort-like houses. It wasn't a good situation, but it wasn't enough to drive people away.

This was the part of the story where the newcomers first heard a name that had stabbed like a knife into the hearts of the Ostfriesen settlers of Texas.

"Comanche," they heard. "Even the women of this tribe are fierce warriors. People say they can gallop hundreds of miles without stopping with every fighter having a string of mounts and changing at the run from horse to horse. You hear about a raid far away on one day; on the next these same warriors can be surrounding your house. They say these warriors can fire their arrows from horseback and hit their target every time, loosing a dozen arrows it the time it takes a man to reload his rifle."

"But." And this was the good part. "Where there are fortifications, the Comanche soon give up and leave. They say they want blood; they mean they want it immediately, otherwise they go where they can find it." Thus the houses of the Saathoffsche Kolonie were walled in stone with gun slits as the only windows.

None of this had been in the letters read during the winter nights in Ludwigsdorf.

But, as Ickka nursed Heinrich and soothed Janna, hoping the fever would pass, they heard of other options for available farm land. There were Ostfriesens living in Waterloo, Illinois, and it was one easy boat ride away.

And on to Illinois

Jann decided on Waterloo. But what about the Frankens? Gerd had signed on to go to Texas with Jann, but he had only

$7.80. That was before paying the boarding house bill. He'd no doubt counted on Jann financing their way right to their Texas destination. Now, if he still wanted to go there? Well, he and his boys could work for wages in New Orleans until they could save enough to cover their travel costs. Manual laborers could earn an incredible $3 an hour in New Orleans, so it wouldn't take long.

But had Gerd considered? If they encountered any unexpected problems and fell into debt? Well, the sight of men, women, and children being sold on the block as indentured servants was sobering. Indentures, even as a way of paying off debt, more often than not meant virtual slavery, meant for many a life-long sentence.

Which was moot. It's likely that none of them wanted to split up their little group. They would do better together. Plus, it's also likely that the Frankens had developed a habit of following Jann's lead. If Jann said they should stay with him, they would. So, Jann paid their fares up river (cost $2.50 per adult and $1.25 per child).

Of course there were dangers and risks associated with steamboat passage, too, and just as fellow travelers had warned of the dangers in Texas, people in the New Orleans boarding house were only too happy to provide tales of horror about river travel.

"Why," they most likely heard, "only a week ago, a packet didn't reach as far as the next turn in the river. There, where the entire of New Orleans could see, the boat simply blew up with bits of bodies strung through the trees on both shores. These things happen, you see. The captain wishes to make a big show of speed, his men overload the boilers, and, that's the end. They say the alligators feasted that night. Well. There was a lot of food for them … 345 men, women, and children. And, that's the truth."

That was the truth. Still, weighing out the relative dangers, Jann booked passage and loaded his charges onto a side-wheel paddle boat, a packet that was a marvel and an incredible treat to the sea-weary, bedraggled immigrants. She looked like something from a fairy tale by the Brothers Grimm, painted in white and red with gilt gingerbread trim on her three decks. The way her huge side wheel turned reminded them of the sails of a windmill. The boat's wheel cut water and propelled the vessel forward, the windmill's sails cut the air and turned the huge grist stones. Both supplied power.

There was something about the packet that invited outlandish ideas. Her stacks blew bellowing clouds of smoke, the Mississippi rippled in her wake, ladies walked her decks in watered satins, the fabric almost a reflection of the river, and crystal chandeliers glittered in the first-class salon. Every inch of her first-class passenger accommodations was intended for comfort and entertainment, something the immigrants could enjoy only from a distance. Which they did.

It was a new world for them. Every bend of the river brought something new and different. Above all, there was speed. Night or day, the packet fairly flew along the surface of the river. Who could imagine such a thing? For the first time, they saw that this truly was a promised land.

In less than a week, the Buss and Franken families travelled almost a thousand miles. To think! While their cheap tickets meant they were sleeping in dormitory space, they had fresh air. There was no limit on fresh water, and no problem with hanging blankets for privacy. Such luxury. If it wasn't for Janna's continued fever, Ickka might have felt worry-free. Even the heat seemed less intense here on the river where there was always a breeze created by their passage. Surely, Janna would soon be back to normal and running about with the other children.

By the second day, they all knew they were in the midst of a once-in-a-lifetime experience. For people whose idea of "pleasure" was limited, whose days for almost every day of their lives had been filled with dawn to dusk work, the riverboat wrought magic. They were as good as on holiday. If it hadn't been for worries about Janna.

Then there was the food, some of which was unfamiliar. There was a vegetable called okra that they all found slimy. Rice had been a rare treat at home but, they learned, was common here and was served with most of their meals. Potatoes might have suffered a blight in Europe but were on the menu. Other vegetables were fresh and plentiful. Best of all, the packet's decks did not roll and pitch as the ship's had, and they could eat without worrying about keeping their dinners down.

No one was seasick and, except for Janna who remained in the sleeping area tossing with intermittent fever, the children could care for themselves. Well, there was Heinrich, who needed attention. He was trying to crawl and needed close watching, a duty Elsche Catharina no doubt was given.

It's difficult to imagine the impact of the trip on Ickka. For the first and last time in her life, she saw, up close, how the wealthy lived. The first-class cabins were set apart, of course, as were the first-class dining room and lounge. But there were good views to be had of those people as they walked the deck and spoke to each other. And who could help peering through the windows of the fabulously appointed first-class lounge? And the women. What a profusion of lace and feathers and shimmering fabrics. What elaborately coifed hair. What delicate little shoes. As for the men? They looked like arrogant peacocks with their silk ties and ridiculous top hats, gold-headed canes, and diamond stickpins.

These people weren't at all like her. Did she close her mind to the incongruity? Or was there envy and bitterness? Maybe. Our only clue is that when she could finally afford fine silks and satins she indulged only in bits of lace to enliven the practical fabrics that made up her wardrobe. In fact she would go out of her way to keep her lifestyle extraordinarily simple.

Thus, she probably concluded—somewhere between her arrival in New Orleans and docking in Quincy, Illinois—that the world was a very strange place indeed with room for all kinds of people and bizarre lifestyles. She'd been brought up isolated from these, and, except for this small exposure, isolated she would stay.

She would also have noted the absence of people or houses along kilometer after kilometer of shore where she saw an occasional deer drinking in the shallows, may have spotted a cougar sleeping on a thick tree branch, and seen an eagle with its white head perched in a dead tree. She would have been amazed when the skies darkened with geese, so many of them that it seemed they would envelope the earth, smothering all other life, the flap of their wings and their shrill calls drowning out all other sound. Did she also marvel at the then common sight of a buffalo herd, the great beasts with their shaggy heads jostling for space along a bank as they came for water?

It was new, and the stories were true about the wild life. This was a land so rich with game that no one need go hungry. We can be sure that Ickka, as with all of them, suffered from sensory overload. So they would take comfort in each other and the sound of their own language even when it was nearly lost in the harsh, loud tones of the land and these strange peoples.

Then, Janna's fever spiked, but this time it didn't drop.

8
Adams County, 1848

On May 27, 1848, the side-wheeler carrying the Buss and Franken families left the main channel of the Mississippi, churned toward the right bank, and entered "the bay" at Quincy, Illinois, finding there a sheltered harbor formed by an island and a peninsula. The great boilers of their packet bled off steam, the captain blew the ship's horn once more to announce their arrival, and the paddlewheel slowed and stopped.

The small town before them was nothing like the cities they had seen downstream.

"Praise be to God," Jann might well have said aloud, the sight of the village lifting his spirits in spite of the tragedy of his daughter's death. High, limestone bluffs faced them shining, white and cream and gray, promising good protection for the village in flood years. Neatly built structures, some of them brick, lined the base of the low cliff while the tops of more buildings showed that most of the village was on its crown. The bank immediately in front of the landing held a wide street and cargo sheds. There were no wharfs or piers, just stanchions to hold ropes and keep a riverboat from drifting away.

By no stretch of the imagination could Quincy be seen as anything except a quiet little village on the edge of the wilderness, but it appeared to be a prosperous enough place in an idyllic setting. Trees with their roots in the spring flood, some of them flowering, crowned the island that formed the outer arm of "the bay." The peninsula, a north-south arm of land, was heavily forested. More trees and vines spilled off the limestone bluffs which were cut by, as seen from the packet's mooring, three ravines. Each of these held a roadway connecting the riverfront to the village on top.

A large shed just north of the landing opened out on the water. The new arrivals would already have heard about it. "That would be their boat works," someone would have said, "Where these Quincy folks built that hull." In St. Louis they had seen an unpainted hull being fitted with its superstructure. "It's a good market," they'd been told. "You can't build steamboats fast enough, so we're trying something new. They're doing the hulls up there in Quincy, float them down, and we'll finish them off here. This is the first."

A sizeable crowd of men and boys would have gathered around the landing as the gangplank, one with hand-railings, swung out from the side of the boat. The road between the landing and a group of sheds to the south would have been busy with wagons, horses, men and boys. A freight wagon may have been descending through a ravine just in front of them, the driver standing on the brake to keep his wagon from overrunning his horses. Muscular arms hauled on four sets of traces, sawing the jaws of the horses almost back to their chests as the wagon nipped at the haunches of the wheel team. "Ho. Ho," they would have heard the man's voice, amplified by the sides of the cut. "Hold, you sons of Satan."

Already the immigrants could see that this town would have the supplies they would need, and Jann was hopeful of buying land somewhere close. They hadn't intended to come this far north, of course. But they'd been side-tracked from Waterloo just as they had from Texas. When they'd reached St. Louis, their disembarkation point for Waterloo, they'd heard that there were Ostfriesens there but also that the available land was both swampy and subject to collapsing in massive sinkholes. Swamps they could handle. Sinkholes?

On the other hand, not much further north, "Good land is maybe four dollars an acre. Very bad land is almost free. And there are Germans there." They also heard that, "The government land office is in Quincy, and all bounty land claims and dispositions will be registered there. You can ask of the government agent, as well."

As the side-wheeler tied up in Quincy, Jann might have wondered if this little town might prove as disappointing as his first two possible destinations. If he felt depressed and pessimistic or worried that they'd again find themselves misled, he can be forgiven. He'd not only had two bad experiences but little Janna had died—and, certainly, that could have been taken as a harbinger of worse things to come.

But he didn't have time to dwell on that. Right now her little body needed to be brought ashore for a Christian burial. And so the party disembarked to face the formalities of arriving with a body, which was no easy thing.

In these years death traveled the river and came ashore off the river boats. Epidemics raged up one side of the river and down the other. The big fear was cholera. Could Janna have died of the dread cholera? Could the packet be infected and spreading its infections as the passengers disembarked?

Jann would have learned the English word "cholera." Everyone knew the dread name of a disease that spread remorsefully and wiped out whole towns and communities. Everyone feared the disease and treated any ship suspected of carrying it as anathema.

"Cholera." Where the possibility arose, fear followed.

In this case, even though telegraph lines had not yet connected St. Louis and Quincy, it's possible that news of the dead child and the cause of death had reached Quincy ahead of the boat. Certainly, word that there were Ostfriesen families aboard the packet preceded it.

Thus, a young man named Johann Kurk appeared and introduced himself to the new arrivals. To the immigrants he was a Godsend—a man who spoke their language, understood their needs, and was a part of this new community.

Johann looked nothing like the angel he seemed to the Buss and Franken families. His arm and leg muscled bulged, built into impressive size by his job as a brickmaker, a job that gave him a good cash income while his father farmed in nearby Clayton Township.

Johann Gerdes Kurk, the father, had come from Schale, near Munster in Westphalia, was a success story himself, and the first German farmer in the area that would eventually be known as South Prairie. Upon his arrival two years earlier, he'd purchased a quarter of a section for $160 or one dollar an acre. Four months after the land purchase his daughter married, and Johann Kurk divided his acreage with his new son-in-law.

As young Kurk told the story to Jann Buss and Gerd Franken over the next few days, all was well for the first year. Then his father and brother-in-law learned they had mistakenly located their homes and had started farming on land they didn't actually own. Fortunately the man who did have legal title was willing to sell. Kurk and his son-in-law, Carl Friedrich Heinecke from Oznabruck in Lower Saxony, purchased and again divided 160 acres for another $160, giving each man a farm of 80 acres, which was considered to be quite a large property. But now they had an excess of 160 acres of untouched prairie—their original purchase—land they needed to sell.

Would Jann and Gerd be interested in buying this for a good price?

To Jann the idea of owning 160 acres was a dream. Who would believe the day might arrive when he could claim to be master of such a huge domain? Even in America? He had already learned that farms of around forty acres or less was the norm. Even in America 160 acres was big.

With Janna buried and his wife, infant son, and remaining daughter settled in a boarding house, Jann determined to see this land for himself.

Accordingly, he set out with his six-year-old son, Gerd. *Where the Wind Blows* by local Golden historian, Anna Wienke, tells us what they saw as they walked up the river then cross-country past farms that helped Jann envision what might someday be his and over undeveloped land he might dream to own.

"… on this prairie untouched by civilization … Violets smiled from under the first grass and strawberry blossoms promised an abundance of the sweet fruit. Wild roses, lilies, woodbine, sunflowers—countless number of almost all kinds of flowers adorned the fields until autumn. The prairie lark hovered over the same and trilled its song. Besides the bees the small, quick hummingbird always found the honey cup of flowers filled. Toothqueen and swallows made a lively and happy bid for friendship. Titmice, finch, thrush, woodpeckers in many varieties, as also a large number of other birds, encouraged the colonists not to be so worried but to be happy and look to the future trusting in God."

Jann was seduced. Yet, he was not blind to the disadvantages. The prairie sod on this slightly undulating, indeed seemingly flat land, gave under the weight of horse and man and would barely support the wheels of a wagon. The surface might be beautiful, a great flowering sea, but the water table was so high that it actually was a sea of sorts or, at a minimum, a lightly disguised swamp.

So, he walked the ground the Kurks had for sale during the days and sat by night listening to Kurk and his son-in-law talking about farming techniques.

"There is enough slope to the ground," they probably told him. And, "A man like you from Ostfriesland knows how to drain the soil to take advantage of the humus. Why there is no limit to how much this farm could produce, never needing fertilizer or replenishment. Here is true black gold, needing only a man to break the sod and plant the seeds. After that some tillage to control weeds, then comes the harvest. Even no harrowing."

Jann wanted to know about relations between the new German settlers and the English, some of whom had been in the township for a generation, long enough to become completely entrenched. "We are on the frontier," Johann would have answered. "We all help each other. Although no one is close, you will not lack for good neighbors. Also, while few of the Englishers are Lutheran, this matter of every man practicing his own religion in America is true. Here we are Presbyterian and Methodist and Lutheran, even Catholic." He dropped his voice. "They say there will be a Jewish synagogue in Quincy one day soon. Imagine."

Some things Jann did not need to ask. There would be disease here, his senses told him. The prairie, for all its grasses and beauty, exuded a foul odor of decay when penetrated by a spade or where bison had wallowed. The air swarmed with insects, and a man in repose without benefit of smoke from a fire soon found his skin a mass of bites, welts, and sores.

As a prudent businessman, Jann spent time in the surrounding villages talking to others with land for sale and about prices. Even though forewarned in Quincy, these were not as good as they had been a few years before, and he could find no trophy lands available for the $10 per hundred acres price some had said he might pay.

While in the hamlet of Clayton, after which Clayton Township was named, he did find one interesting proposition. The Clayton Township School Trustees owned a piece of land which had been seized from a previous owner for nonpayment of taxes. Proceeds from the sale of this land were to be used to build a school. The Trustees told Jann they would be willing to let the land go for a very small down payment, financing the $150 price over ten years. This land had the advantage of having been partially cleared. It also had a small log structure. A family could move straight in and begin farming.

But Jann was in love with the idea of a larger property and continued looking. Finally, after several weeks, beguiled by the Kurk property but, additionally, to news that the railroad line to Springfield would pass not far from that land, he returned to the Kurks. After considerable bargaining, he settled for $1.55 per acre for the 160 acre plot or $248. He also made arrangements with one of the English neighbors to buy what he called a "block" house. It was a 20-by-30 foot log structure built some thirty years earlier as a first home. The original owners had sold it to newcomers when they constructed their first real house. The Buss family would be the third family to use it.

"Now," he told Johann Kurk, "I must return to Quincy to buy what we will need here and to bring my family to this place."

Jann and six-year-old Gerhard, mostly walking, made the thirty-plus mile trip in two days. In the early afternoon of the second day, they reached the outermost edge of Quincy, then twelfth street, coming in along Vermont Avenue. Perhaps a wagon gave them a ride on this last stretch of their journey, possibly one laden with vegetables headed for the market and jouncing along the rutted and overgrown track.

The town was by this time platted with numbered streets paralleling the leading edge of the bluff over the Mississippi, the numbered streets bisected by named ones with the business portion of the town and most of the development grouped around the main square between 4th and 5th Streets. While the streets Jann traveled had yet to be paved and the rough structures along them were far from beautiful or more than utilitarian, it was now June and at least the way was dry if dusty.

As he approached the main square, the buildings began to show Quincy as the prosperous town it was. Glass gleamed in windows, walls glowed with the rosy tones of brick, and grew to two and three stories in height. Sidewalks, even, marched along the edges of streets paved in stones.

No one waited for the two Buss males with open or any other kind of arms although all five Frankens plus Ickka and Elsche Catharina had remained behind. It's possible that Ickka and Gesche had gotten jobs, as many immigrant women did, doing piece work for a garment maker. It would have given them pocket money while providing an occupation during this period of waiting and a means for meeting other women.

While we can't tell for sure what the women did during this interval, the Franken men had definitely found employment, thanks again to the young Kurk. They had well-paying jobs laboring on a new bridge being built across the river near

Quincy, joining other men before dawn every day to hike out to the bridge site, taking their lunches and dinners—tied into a scrap of cloth—with them. While they did not reappear until the late-setting June sun was low in the sky, they were satisfied. Only the heat bothered them.

"Imagine all of us earning such good wages," would have been Gerd Franken's dominant feeling, one he probably shared with Jann when his brother-in-law returned from looking for land.

It's probable that a work and heat-weary Gerd stayed up until well after dark the night that Jann reappeared, enjoying the cool damp and the flashes of lightning bugs as darkness gathered around them. The two men might have held lit pipes, which would have been a luxury they could now afford, one that went with their new American home. And the two men would have had much to discuss about the future. What they did next would affect the rest of their lives.

Gerd and Gesche

During Jann's absence, Gerd would've figured out that by the time the bridge was built the salaries he and his boys earned, even with living costs subtracted, would provide enough to return what they owed Jann and to make a down payment on land. Then, the boys could remain in Quincy with paying jobs while Gerd began farming. He might even have shared a glowing thought, "With the boy's wages and farm income we will soon be as prosperous as the richest farmers at home."

More, Gerd would have had time and opportunity to consult with many other men about this new land, about the opportunities. Just because a family arrived poor did not mean they needed to stay that way. Just because they had low status in Ostfriesland, did not mean they would have low status here.

But the dreams and plans percolating through Gerd's thoughts may not have received a sympathetic hearing from Jann Buss. He had other ideas for the Frankens.

Even before he'd purchased so much property, he'd known it would take more than one pair of hands to farm it. When he'd made it possible for the Frankens to emigrate and counted out payment for his new farm, he'd certainly also counted on one or more of the Franken males working alongside him. Now? Without them?

Then there was the question of what Gerd Franken could actually do. Jann may well have had a completely different view of Gerd's prospects than Gerd, himself. At forty-seven, as we've noted, Gerd was old by the standards of the time. How much longer would his working life last? He might be a tough old bird who didn't complain about his joints or old injuries, but there was this thing of ambition and follow-through. Yes, Gerd had gotten himself and his family to America, but, otherwise, he'd never been a particularly enterprising man, had been satisfied to take work where he found it. His one piece of major luck in his life had been in marrying Gesche. Now, thanks largely again to that luck, he was in a new land … making his own plans.

But that said, he was the same man Jann had known all his life—a good man, a hard-working man, but not the sort to strike out on his own. No. Jann needed the Frankens in Clayton Township, and he needed them there right away.

Which brings us to the school land. Jann might have thought of it as just the attraction that would get Gerd to

Clayton Township. The trustees would sell it on time. Jann could provide the down-payment. Gerd, his boys, and Jann could immediately begin farming in order to get crops on both their properties before winter. As for day labor in Quincy? There was no time for that. Not this summer, anyway. When winter came, perhaps. Yes. When winter came Gerd and his boys could return to Quincy to earn money.

From Gerd's point of view, this plan had flaws. By winter the bridge work might not be available. Besides, it was all well and good for Jann to advance money for a down payment. But Gerd would still need cash to buy seed, a cow and a plow, some chicks, food for at least six weeks and, most of all, a gun. With a gun, he would always have something for the cooking pot.

Apparently, the men compromised. Gerd and the boys would remain in Quincy, possibly planning on staying just long enough to earn money for supplies, chickens, a milk cow … that sort of thing. Gesche and their daughter, Antje, would go with the Buss family and set up housekeeping, the women getting gardens established to ensure winter supplies.

Did anyone ask Gesche Buss Franken what she thought or wanted? Had anyone ever asked her? Nonetheless, she knew she would probably outlive her husband by a fair number of years. She knew she might have to either remarry or struggle to provide for her children. What her man decided now would be critical to that future. And there were these assumptions of Jann's—ones he would not have made if her husband enjoyed more respect. Gesche knew all about that, having never had it. She'd been kept at home long after the normal marriage age, been treated like a servant by her own parents, been married off to an older man below her family's economic status, then been at the bottom of the pecking order ever since. She'd been jerked out of that life, survived two dreadful months, been exposed to amazing wealth and diversity, and now this. She had never known a day of independence … then came Quincy.

She and Ickka lived in a boarding house exposed daily to these American women and their ideas. As mentioned, they may even have gotten temporary work and seen an entirely new kind of life; met single women who were neither prostitutes nor servants but strong, independent individuals. What did that do to Gesche? For one thing, she'd seen jobs come and go in Gerd's life. Each new one had seemed good, but none had lasted long. Land on the other hand? Pray God Gerd lived long enough or her boys stayed close to home. If that happened, they could own this schoolhouse land outright. She would have it forever.

As for Ickka, she must have been relieved to see her little Gerhard return tanned and healthy and full of stories about their travels. She would have been more than pleased that Jann had found land and so much land! The size of the holding and her husband's plans for keeping the Frankens close to them no doubt also made her happy. She needed people she knew around her, people who shared her personal history and values, who spoke her language and thought in the same way as she did. And the land? The more land she and Jann owned, the safer and more secure her family would be.

But at what cost? Already she had endured more than she had thought it possible for people to survive. Even the hardships of her childhood, the want and deprivation, the desperate cold, the feelings of helplessness had not prepared her for what Jann had put them through. Very few men risked their young children to these and dozens of other dangers. Yet, Jann had, and Janna had died.

Well. Ickka had learned a thing or two during the voyage. The Ickka Eilerts Buss who left Ludwigsdorf some four months earlier was not the same woman Jann faced when he returned from his property search.

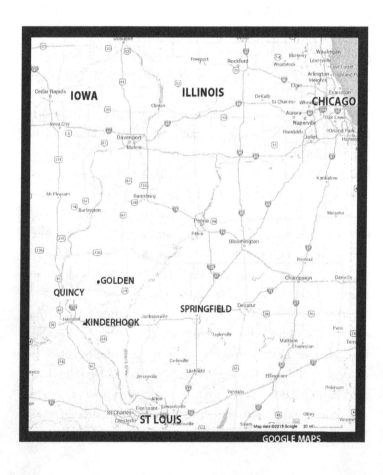

9
Quincy, 1848

B ack in Quincy from his land search, Jann began what was likely the biggest shopping spree of his life, one that echoed in reverse the auction of his possessions fifteen months earlier. Without doubt, he was as prepared as was possible for this record day. It's likely he'd devoted hours to an exploration of Quincy's stores, checking advertisements in the newspaper, and talking to people. Certainly, he'd had the advantage of the many letters home that had listed going prices for everything from yard goods to barrels. So, using his undoubtedly prodigious memory—one honed on mentally inventorying, tracking, and accounting for the goods he'd carried up and down the canals of Ostfriesland— he would now have finalized the Bill of Materials for his new farming enterprise and probably knew, almost to a penny, what he would spend.

One of his major concerns about this shopping binge would have been language. Some might interpret his poor English as ignorance. They might view him as an easy mark, might try to overcharge him or unload inferior goods on him. Even without the language barrier, of course, that could happen, hence his preparation which no doubt included identifying and researching the reputations of the local German merchants. He would've used them by preference where possible.

Thus he set out. We can see him striding along Quincy's streets and by-ways with determined steps and a gleam in his eyes. Yet, even with all his homework, would he have had a few doubts weighing down his feet, acting as lead weights on his confidence?

Horses. If he was particularly worried about anything, it would've been horses. Every American—almost every American male—owned at least one horse. It appears that Jann, having lived on the water, knew little about these animals even though many of his fellow countrymen were great horsemen and horse breeders. But not Jann.

He doubtlessly did, however, know the downside of horse ownership. Equines could be dangerous. They were unpredictable. They suffered numerous health and lameness problems. And the big concern? Even experts could be made fools of by these princes among con men—these horse traders.

If he was worried, he had good cause because he ended up purchasing what we can guess from subsequent events was an aged animal, probably also one of poor quality. Likely, too, he had no idea of the fact at the time of purchase.

"Ten years old and I've had him the whole time. Never been lame a day in its life and so gentle the children ride him." So goes the horse trader's pitch, then and now. "Look at those legs, clean as a whistle, no blemishes, no swelling, no problems. Look at those shoulders. Strong and upright. They'll pull a plow or a wagon all day long. Why I've owned Laddy here since he was weaned. He's plumb gentle. Never give you a moment of trouble."

No doubt the gelding he did buy was well-groomed, his coat polished with an oiled cloth. He would not have recognized bowed tendons or spavin or any of the long list of puffy or out of alignment ailments that plague older animals. Upright shoulders? How could Jann be expected to know that such shoulders create a jarring gait and subject the animal to more lameness. What he did know was he had much to learn if he was to own horses. And in this land at this time? He had no choice. He had to buy a horse.

So he did.

Guns were another matter and an equally important purchase. Not only did every frontier family own at least one gun, the quality of the gun would make a difference. In this matter, we can assume, Jann knew what he was doing—marksmanship being a prized skill among the Ostfriesens.

Once his purchases were made, Jann could now consider himself a man among men, the owner of a gun, a horse, and an estate large enough to befit a nobleman. We can only imagine how he felt about all of this. Elation? Pleasure? Trepidation?

What else did he buy?

His shopping list certainly would have included everything he wouldn't be able to find in the hamlets close to his property plus other things that were just cheaper in Quincy. Specifically, he probably traded in his wooden clogs for a pair of stout leather boots. Then there were farm implements and farm animals. Some of these would have come from neighbors, others he would have trailed with him, perhaps a heifer or two, a bred milk cow with calf, a few spring lambs, and a litter of pigs. He would need seed, feed for the animals, and a three-month supply of staples for his household.

Ickka would have to have a loom to replace the one sold at home and … imagine! Cotton—a fabric that cost the moon at home—was affordable and made for lighter-weight clothes to match the summer climate. He would buy the yardage. Ickka would make them new clothes. Then there were other household items like a butter churn and milking buckets, like a large copper tub for washing clothes and humans.

Chickens and goslings probably came from the neighbors, but he would need bundles of shingles, which most would consider a luxury. But Jann had heard a great deal about the roofing problems that went with log cabins, like the one he'd purchased. He would've wanted to make it tight against the winter storms.

"This is the problem with these block houses," men would probably have said. "With flat plank roofs rain comes through and in the winter snow piles up. Sometimes the roof collapses. If not, it leaks, melting snow being as bad as weeks of rain. Either way the floor is all the time mud which is bad for the health of the family." Also, "Many people die only because of bad humors from the floor. Even though there are these stout walls, the roof is no good, and the results?"

No. It would be necessary to put a slant roof on his block house and cover it with shingles.

In the meantime, Gerd had been doing his own shopping. With almost three weeks' salary in hand, he had been able to buy essential items for his women folk—things like garden implements, seed, and food supplies. There was a little cabin on the property where Gesche and Antje would live until they could afford something better. And, with the women gone, Gerd and his boys could live rough, thereby saving more money.

Thus the Buss-Franken party, diminished by three, set forth, soon reaching Quincy's outer edge at 12th Street on Vermont. They continued along Vermont's wide and rutted dirt track. At what would become 24th Street, Vermont narrowed and, soon, they found themselves walking on torn-up grass and ruts, small shrubs and saplings trying to grow under their feet. Quincy disappeared behind them, hidden by trees and the rise and fall of the land. They were well on their way.

While poorly maintained, the route was well-travelled here, was visible as ruts that snaked through forest lands, across clearings and up and down the many cuts made by creeks that fed the Mississippi and bisected their northerly travel. "The way is hard on axels," they'd been told, "but you will not lose the track between here and Camp Point. There you follow one of the trails east." Jann, of course, had been this way before and knew what to expect.

It was getting on to the middle of June, now. What had been a long winter and a cold, wet spring had yielded to summer, finally giving the land's vegetation a proper growing environment. Everywhere the countryside demonstrated its determination to make up for lost time. Everywhere Ickka saw validation of Jann's decision to relocate to this fertile and abundant country.

What gave plant life an ideal medium, though, created human suffering, especially for those raised in a cold climate and still wearing clothing appropriate to their homeland. Sweat gathered along the band of Jann's hat, under his belt, and soaked his shirt. It pulled wet strands of hair from under the women's caps, ones that lacked even a rudimentary bill or brim to shade the face. Then, too, the women wore wooden clogs which chafed their swollen feet until both Ickka and Gesche probably took them off to walk barefoot, like the children.

Baby Heinrich, more than likely, was confined to a box placed under the wagon's seat, perhaps with a cloth tented over it. He would have been sitting up now and crawling and no longer content to lie placidly waiting for his mother to nurse him. Thus, it's likely that Ickka had created makeshift toys, possibly bits of knotted rag and sanded wood. Heinrich might also have had smooth joint bones to chew on and help the teething process. All of this for a boy nearly seven months old would do little to prevent fussy behavior, and his protests no doubt followed the party. Poor little soul. So far his life had been one moment of dislocation and misery after another.

It was just too hot and humid. Even when the track took them under the shady branches of trees what they gained in a slight drop in temperature was lost in comfort by the swarms of insects that found any inch of exposed skin irresistible. Bugs, heat, and a baby's crying does not make for a pleasant stroll across country.

Still they all had reason to be happy or at least pleased. Finally, they were on the last leg of their journey. Soon, they would reach the long-promised land.

During the first day's march, they may have seen an amazing sight, one that brought them to a standstill, caused them to stop and stare. The new telegraph was being extended north of Quincy at the time of the Buss journey and was being strung along the same path. Giant wooden spools wound with wire would have stood on the ground and reached higher than their wagon wheels. Perhaps they even passed a camp housing the telegraph stringers, one complete with sleeping shelters, a big cook tent, lines of work horses or oxen used to transport the telegraph poles, big wagons, and the wire. The family would have heard the shouts of men, the creaks of wagons, the sharp cracks as trees fell. They may even have stopped to share a meal and marvel at the changes coming to their new neighborhood.

Whether they approved or not was another matter.

The Last Leg

They no doubt reached Camp Point while it was still light. Jann and young Gerhard would have met one or more

Plattdeutsch-speaking families here on their earlier expedition and might even have made arrangements to board the entire family overnight on the way back through, a practice normal in the area.

Likely, they ate a hearty meal of beans seasoned with bacon plus cornbread—the same hospitality they would soon be expected to offer to any traveler landing on their own doorsteps at the end of a day. Just as likely they slept head to toe in a row on a blanket-softened board floor much as they had slept on their platforms aboard the *Elizabeth*.

The next morning they would have tried for an early start. Leaving the few shops, houses, and trees of Camp Point, they drove onto a flat inland sea of grass. Soon, as far as they could see in any direction, grass waved in the omnipresent prairie breeze. While hot and uncomfortable at this time of year, it kept the insects down and would have been welcome.

To these Ostfriesens it was a bit like being on the ocean but without the waves. Perhaps they compared it to their own homeland … if they could only add the canals and their snug houses.

Yet, the differences were more striking than the similarities. Here, shallow sinks held trickles of water where masses of berry bushes grew, the raspberries thick on the vine and ready to eat. Small animals darted out of their path. Larger game, wary of the passing party, moved away from them. There was undulation to the ground, but you couldn't see it. They could look ahead to a flat monotony but come suddenly upon a pond or rivulet and clumps of bushes. Then, looking back, they could watch these features disappear, seemingly swallowed up by the vast nothingness.

The wagon rolled along, most likely averaging two miles

an hour or less, due to the many types of impedances—like having to lever it both up and down banks to cross the little rivulets; like the time it took to free mired wheels. As dry as the weather was, the thick turf underfoot felt spongy beneath their feet. No wonder the wagon sank into it again and again. Again and again, the horse strained. Jann applied the whip, the women unloaded the heavier items, then reloaded them. Baby Heinrich cried. Chickens drowsed in their crates. The wheels turned and dug themselves into the prairie. The girls, Elsche Catharina and Antje, hot in their woolens, sunburned and scratching at bug bites, knew better than to whine but lagged behind.

Also, there was the smell, almost one of rotten eggs.

"It is the prairie," they'd been told. "Soon you will not notice, and when you do you will think it is the smell of the ground making fertilizer for itself and food for your family."

The prairie. The land hit the senses as hard as a slap in the face. The colors were intense and shifting, never quite the same from hour to hour. And noise? The wind blew, swishing through the grasses, moaning along the sunken waterways. Insects made whirring sounds, sometimes so loud they drowned out the songbirds or the cries of raptors and made it difficult to hear yourself think. Never was there silence or simply the gentle lap of water against land. This America was extravagant, unfamiliar, and disorienting.

No more so than at night when the stars came out. This was not the muted and distant night sky Ickka knew at home. Here the sky enveloped them, wrapping them in arms of darkness. Even in Quincy, they had noticed that as soon as the sun went down a few stars would prick the pale blue and yellow evening sky. With full dark, millions more sprang to life in such abundance that even the vast prairie sky couldn't seem to hold them, and they elbowed and jostled, clustering and glowing and creating an altogether new world of grays and blacks edged in silver.

Cutting through everything would come the hooting of owls or the howl of some beast, a sound like nothing they had heard before, a sound that frightened the children and reminded the adults of stories from the old days when, they said, wolves came down out of the far north and stole babies from the houses. And every mile travelled brought more signs of just how wild and different this land was, made it abundantly clear they were in a totally foreign place where they didn't know the rules and where anything—probably an anything bad—could happen at any moment.

10
The First Accident, 1848

Jann and Ickka had all the materials they needed to raise their log cabin. Of course, a dismantled 500-square feet structure without floor, foundation, interior walls, and with only a sloping roof was a simple proposition. Even so, neither Jann nor Ickka had any need or desire to build their house by themselves.

Shortly after their arrival in what they were now calling South Prairie, word circulated around Clayton Township (where the good land had been settled by English-speaking Americans some thirty years earlier) about the new German-speaking family who'd bought a large piece of swampy prairie from the Kurks. A house-raising would provide an excellent opportunity to get the measure of these new folks.

The Americans here had been pioneers who valued team efforts and practiced hospitality. They weren't people who were accustomed to 'foreigners,' but they knew about the Germans who had a reputation as thrifty and hard-working. It helped, too, that the Kurks had demonstrated those qualities and were widely admired for, among other things, the way Johann had made right his accidental settlement on land that wasn't his. Those things did happen; it was the way a man resolved the situation that counted. More, many of the men of Clayton Township had met Jann on his property-buying trip and knew—more likely from the Kurks than from Jann—that these particular German-speakers came from an area reclaimed from the North Sea and were experienced in water and drainage engineering. Perhaps, the neighbors speculated, these newcomers could turn the land that others had spurned into something useful? At any event, it'd be interesting to watch and see what happened.

And in the meantime, "lending a neighborly hand" would give everyone a day off. Yes. There would be a cabin-raising. And the timing was right. The crops had all been planted; the first hay cutting was finished. It was the mid-season lull during which farmers played catch-up. No one minded a break from the kinds of chores that filled these days.

Thus, farm families began to arrive with their teams of horses and wagons loaded with tools and children. Ickka would probably have been warned by Johann Kurk's wife about what to expect and would have been ready with trestle tables (probably made from saw horses and roof planks) lined up near the place where Jann intended to situate his house.

We know that Jann had completed at least one property-owner's project before this day, something the neighbors would note as their teams pulled up to the site, passing a peculiar sort of gate. It consisted of a single long pole balanced on a fulcrum. "It is of a type used in our home," Jann probably explained. "Now, any of my countrymen coming this way will know this place belongs to an Ostfriesen."

It was a gesture of hope—hope that other Ostfriesens would come, hope that the Buss farm would be a core around which other Ostfriesens would gather. God willing, they would come. God willing, they would bring their language and customs, and they would establish an Ostfriesen community in the midst of this English-speaking land.

And so, on that seminal day the neighbors passed the open bar, women and girls jumping down from their wagons in what would be a yard, their hands holding covered dishes. The wagons then wheeled around and disappeared down the track toward a nearby forested area where the blockhouse had been disassembled and waited transport. When they returned, the wagon beds were piled with notched logs, the bones of the block house Jann had purchased on his earlier trip.

By noon, the men would have moved all the logs and poles while others had staked and cleared the ground and begun the reassembly. Most of them had done this a number of times before. In fact, they may have handled these same logs, recycling them each time a family had the wherewithal to build a frame house. Thus, we can assume they were well along with their work when they broke for their mid-day dinner.

Did Ickka appreciate the help? Maybe not so much. She could well have been terrified in the presence of these foreigners who spoke an incomprehensible language, who practiced customs she did not understand and brought food she didn't recognize. Until a few short months earlier, she'd never met anyone who spoke a language she didn't understand. In fact, she'd seldom encountered even one person unknown to her or her family, let alone dozens.

And, dear God, how strange they were. From her first day in New Orleans, Ickka would have recognized that Americans were different. They were loud and boisterous and outspoken. The women talked over the top of each other and their men. No one seemed to listen. They just talked. Plus their words came so fast and ran together in such a way that Ickka couldn't even pick out the few English words she'd memorized. She couldn't even understand the words that were the same … just sounded different.

The strangest thing about these Americans, though, was their body language. They used extravagant gestures, their arms making great circles in the air, their hands waving like the sails of a windmill. They talked, in fact, as though they were engaged in a constant game of charades. Unfortunately Ickka understood the body language no better than the English.

The worst thing, though, was where they put themselves relative to her. They all seemed to want lots of space around their bodies as though they had to spread out and fill the land just to carry on a conversation. No one moved close to talk and, when Ickka tried to edge nearer to create a companionable space, the woman would back away as though in fear.

Yet no one could fault their generosity and friendly, open-arms attitudes. She'd already learned that every farm on the frontier was more or less obligated to take in passing travelers for the night, to feed them and find a dry, safe place for them to sleep. No one could fault the goodness of their hearts toward fellow pioneers even though they might be a bit frightening in their habits.

That day, as the men transported and raised a block house for the Buss family complete with a low, slanting, plank roof, Ickka probably thought she had seen the best in her neighbors. She was wrong.

Dennis Miller in "Der Muller's Sohn" picks up the tale here: "The next day Jan Buss and his wife Ikke (sic) took the old wagon and old horse they had purchased in Quincy and with a horse borrowed from their neighbor set out with the team of horses to retrieve the rocks for the chimney for the cabin."

Again, Jann and Ickka had help. Several neighbors had returned to lend a hand in finishing the work of the day before by filling the gaping hole they'd left in one end of the 20'x30' cabin.

By now, Ickka had probably adopted the sun bonnet favored

among pioneer women. It's also likely that Ickka would already be known to the neighbor ladies by her nickname, "Moder," a name that soon all would use.

Was it a misunderstanding? Had they heard her family calling Ickka "Moder" (because she was their mother) and jumped to an erroneous conclusion?

The neighbors could be forgiven for finding Ickka's name a bit difficult for their tongues. It was foreign to them. It could be mixed up with the expression "ick," a derogatory. And there was no easy Anglicization. Berendji would become Bertha. Janna would be known as Jenny. Catharina as Cathy. But Ickka? Well. She became Moder.

Moder and Jann Buss rode together on this day. We can imagine Ickka hanging onto her jouncing bench, her face red and sunburned even though now shaded by a bonnet. Both she and her husband would have been sweating, their clothes chaffing their skin and creating rashes. The Illinois summer prairie was just that hot, their German clothing just that unsuitable.

They would have made a lot of noise on their passage, too. Leather harness, axels, wagon wood, all would have squeaked and groaned over the uneven trail. Chain jangled, horse tails swished, and small animals and reptiles had plenty of warning to get out of the way.

Flies were a different matter, swarming around the heads of horses and humans alike. But there were good things, too, for the prairie was a beautiful place, with every step revealing summer flowers hidden in the long grasses or popping out of low bushes. Birds sailed above them, rose from beneath the horses' feet, and sang from coverts.

Eventually, they came to the woodlot where their cabin had once stood and where the rocks they sought were heaped.

What happened here? Was there a gate, and did Jann have to turn the team to go through it? Did Ickka get down to open it for him? Was this Jann's first experience driving a pair of horses?

We know the two animals were mismatched—one old, the other not. Was the younger horse green and poorly trained? Certainly, he or she would not have the experience of Jann's elderly animal and, usually, under these circumstances, the senior suffers very little from the junior. Kicks and bites teach quick lessons in how to behave in harness. In fact it's common practice to pair a young horse with an older one and let the older one do the job of training. Which might have been the idea here, and a good idea on the face of it.

In fact, it could have been a win-win situation. Jann would have the use of a young, strong animal to move his fireplace rock while the owner would get back a more tractable driving horse.

Except it didn't work that way. Was what happened caused by Jann's inexperience with horses? He may never have driven a team. And, while it was essential that he learn, he probably approached the work with trepidation. By this time he certainly knew that horse-related accidents were common and a major cause of non-disease casualties on the frontier. Statistics from the period are hard to come by, but we do have fairly reliable records on what happened along the Oregon Trail where horse-drawn wagon accidents were the leading cause of death. Certainly, anyone who drove or rode a horse knew the dangers. Like cars now, horses then were necessary. They were transportation. They were time and energy savers. But they could kill you.

In any event, Jann was about to get a first-hand lesson. How it happened, we'll never know, but the wagon he was driving hit a tree. Then came something much more agonizing and terrible than a simple wagon wreck, which would have been bad enough.

Out of the bole of the tree came a very obviously and loudly angry swarm of bees. They hung in the air for a moment before their scouts located the threat. The swarm massed and turned in a cloud toward the man and the horses. The horses did what horses do, they obeyed their fright/flight reflexes and ran.

Perhaps Ickka was on the wagon at the time and was thrown off. Or, as conjectured above, perhaps she'd gotten down to open a gate. In any event, the swarm left her alone and concentrated on horses and man.

The empty wagon bed jounced behind the fleeing, desperate horses, probably catching on roots and branches, breaking up as it became hopelessly tangled in the woodlot's undergrowth, the horses then brought to a stop, trapped by their harness, fighting and screaming with pain in their high-pitched terrible way.

The old horse survived, which means his harness most likely broke, and he escaped. Because Jann had purchased old and cracked leather? The young animal, though, was severely stung.

Jann was lucky. The neighborhood women had experience with stings and knew how to make poultices to pull them, which probably relieved some of the pain.

There was no such treatment or possibility for the young horse. Instead, there would've been a bullet to end his misery.

We don't know if Jann was taken to one of the neighbor's homes … his open-ended cabin being little more than a hovel at that point … or what exactly happened. The goodness of the neighbors had already been demonstrated. But no matter how much help they gave, Ickka had to feel lost, frightened, and very alone—vulnerable and overwhelmed—at this sudden turn of fate.

One good thing, the owner of the young horse took Jann's old one as recompense. As a result, Ickka would have no horse, but at least she hadn't added debt to her list of woes.

What did she have as assets? Presuming the neighbors completed her fireplace, she had a cabin with a roof that would leak until covered with shakes. It was equipped with bench beds (the outside posts set in the earthen floor), clothing pegs, and a shelf. She had bedding, a few animals, basic clothing items, the trunks that they had brought with them, Jann's farm equipment purchases and gun, and her pots and pans. She also had the food staples brought from Quincy.

Nothing had worked the way Jann had planned. Instead of two men and three boys to finish the cabin, turn the sod, put in a crop, and build shelters for the animals, there was just her. And how was she to do all of this while, at the same time, nursing Jann and keeping her children and the livestock safe and fed?

If she sat down and cried, she could be forgiven. Six months earlier she'd still been in the beautiful house her parents in-law had built, a place she'd left with promises of a new world of unlimited land and opportunity. Getting here had cost her a daughter and the hell of the sea passage.

Now this.

11
Lord God in Heaven

"The Lord giveth, the Lord taketh away. Blessed be the name of the Lord, Amen."

It was hot out and not much cooler inside. The men of the township had raised the Buss block house, had fetched the rock and, most probably, built their fireplace. They'd also hammered together a few pieces of rudimentary furniture. The roof was up, but rays of sunshine likely shone through the cracks to illuminate the cabin's dusty interior. More light came through the open plank doors, one in front and one in back and the one glassless window opening. Despite the heat, a fire burned in the fireplace.

Sunday dinner simmered in a pot, filling the cabin with a mouth-watering smell. Flies buzzed. Spiders crept about the walls, setting up housekeeping. Outside, chickens made dust nests and tried to stay cool while local birds explored nesting possibilities in the relocated logs.

It was Sunday, the 2nd of July, and it would have been the first of many Sunday services held in that little house. All four German families in South Prairie were there, Gesche and Antje Franken walking from their own small cabin to the Buss block house. We can imagine the children sitting together on a bed platform, a quilt and straw ticking pillowing their bottoms.

Jann would no longer have been in danger of dying from his stings, but he was probably still in pain, his eyes perhaps swollen, his face covered with soothing poultices. Ickka might well have made him as comfortable as possible on another of the platforms by rolling up a quilt and turning it into a bolster.

Being the Lord's Day, the women were in their Sunday best—fabric almost colorless from intense exposure to sea salt and sun. Their Bibles, which were probably the only books to make the journey to the new world, would have been open in their hands. Neither woman was much of a reader, but they'd learned their letters from their parish priests and knew great swatches of scripture and common prayers by heart. Thus, even though Jann might not have been up to the task of reading from the Bible or being a lay service leader, they could manage the task by themselves, the children joining them in songs and prayers of thanks.

They actually had much to be grateful for. So, while the future must have seemed fraught with impossible challenges, for the moment on that Sunday morning it seemed the worst was behind them. Janna was dead, gone to a better place, but none of the rest of them had caught the killing fever. Jann had been seriously injured, but he would recover. The baby, Heinrich, had survived the horrible journey and seemed to be thriving despite the inevitable heat rashes. The other children were in tolerable health.

And to think! Gerd and the Franken boys were earning excellent wages and would soon have enough to pay their first year's mortgage and buy the necessities for their farm. Then, they would all be together again, Gerd and sons helping to prepare the Buss acreage for its first cash crop.

In the meantime, Ickka had no horse and no wagon, but she had herself to pull a plow, which she might well have been doing the last few days, not on the Buss land but on the Franken's.

The women had, of necessity, planted or were in the process of planting a garden. No matter what else might happen the matter of kitchen crops was crucial, and they were already too late to expect a full harvest. Still, depending on when the first frosts came, they'd probably realize an ample bounty—enough to ensure full stomachs for themselves and their animals during the winter months.

Why would the garden have been on the Franken farm? From what we know, the Buss property was all virgin prairie. In essence that meant it consisted of dense, centuries-old soggy networks of roots and warrens descending several feet below the surface. Busting that sod and draining it would be a major effort and way beyond what one woman with a plow or a shovel could do.

Some of the Franken place, on the other hand, had been previously farmed. So, with children in tow, the two women would have laid out a garden, tilled and raked their plot, and put in seeds for basic vegetables and grains. That done, they could think of something more ambitious. Like planting a cash crop.

But first came the day of worship and fellowship.

"Thank you, God, for the blessings of this day and the food we eat."

Yes. They could be grateful but not for long.

"…and the Lord taketh away …"

Gerd Franken, who'd remained behind to work on the Mississippi bridge, was embroiled in a nightmare that Sunday.

It'd all happened because he'd been driven, as he had for most of his life, by a lack of money. Upon arrival in Illinois, he'd committed himself to more debt by contracting to buy the school-held property. Now, he not only had whatever he owed Jann to repay, but he'd taken on a mortgage. Plus, to work the land he would need equipment and supplies and money for taxes, not to mention he still had a family to support. How to handle all of this?

He most likely approached his problems as he had previous ones—on a day to day basis. He would put his head down, go to work every day, and tackle each challenge as he came to it. In the meantime, he was a land owner. When he allowed himself the time to think about it, he must have smiled and felt a glow of pride. He owned as much land as the richest lord back home.

Also, he and his boys were earning good wages laboring on a new bridge over the Mississippi, being paid at a rate unthinkable in Ostfriesland. This new world was every bit as wonderful as he'd been led to believe. When even a poor, older man could realize so many blessings, well … it made you want to kneel down and thank the good Lord.

But bad luck had followed Gerd to America.

The Buss Family of Ostfriesland tells the story, "Gerd and his sons journeyed to the bridge site and immediately began working. On 1 July 1848, Gerd's sons Tjark and Gerd were standing in the vicinity of a rack of massive logs used to build the expansion bridge. Without any warning the log rack collapsed and the rolling logs crushed Tjark and severely injured young Gerd. Other German emigrants at the site worked to free the brothers and assisted their father in returning them home."

Twelve-year-old Tjark died of his injuries. Young Gerd sustained broken bones, including a broken hip—an injury that usually meant a long, prolonged decline to an inevitable death. Thus, on Sunday, the 2nd of July 1848, while his wife was giving thanks for God's blessings, Gerd Franken and unnamed other men were on their way to South Prairie, doubtlessly thinking it was better for the one boy to be buried near the rest of his family and the other boy to die there with his mother.

The trip would have been hell for the nine-year-old as the wagon bumped and bucked across the rough land in what would have been, at best, a two-day trip. He would have drifted in and out of consciousness, would have heard the men discussing his miserable prospects, might have witnessed his father's stoic grief over the departed Tjark and for what he would have seen as the end of his short-lived dreams.

Yes. Gerd Senior nominally had the land, but Gesche's child-bearing days were behind her. Now, there would be no strong sons to help with the farm; no sons to care for Gerd and Gesche in their old age, which was fast approaching. Time was running out.

And the worst of it? What if young Gerd actually did survive? He'd become a bed-ridden burden and a drain on the family's meager assets for so long as he might live.

Hopefully, God was merciful in a small way and someone rode ahead of the funeral party to notify Gesche.

And that was the end of Gesche's dreams, as well. She would have been looking forward to a summer of hard and rewarding work—caring for her six-year-old daughter, turning her new small shack into a home, tending her garden and a few animals, and sharing Sundays with her brother and sister-in-law. With her husband and sons all earning good wages, with her own labor producing the vegetables that would see her family through the winter, Gesche most likely thought the Franken family would be on a sound economic footing come 1849.

Until this.

Whatever the actual circumstances surrounding the return of her remaining menfolk, Gesche rose to the challenge. No matter the degree of her shock and grief, no matter her other worries about feeding herself and her remaining family, when Gerd Jr. arrived she did what was necessary and more than necessary. She accomplished what was nearly impossible in that era. She not only nursed her only remaining son back to health but to mobility. While she was at it, she gave him a trade that would provide him with an income and lead to a modest prosperity. She taught him to sew.

He would always have a permanently deformed hip and one leg shorter than the other. He would lurch more than walk, but he could get around. This Gerd would never be a farmer or a laborer. He would also never know a pain-free day, but the tailor, Gerd Franken, would live until 1902 as a productive and valued member of his community.

Life in America

It was a dreadfully inauspicious beginning, the two deaths and two accidents spiking into the lives of these sons and daughters of Ostfriesland. Besides causing heart-rending grief and unremitting pain, it was a game-changer. Not only did it force a sharp reassessment of everyone's plans, but it immediately transformed everyday life. Gesche lost a son and gained an invalid who needed intense nursing; Gerd lost both the labor and the income of his two boys and was forced to scale back his expectations and increase his already onerous workload. And these latest woes came while Jann was still bed-ridden, his life on hold.

Did they curse their bad luck or their dour God?

If any or all of the adults felt despair over the decision to emigrate and fell into debilitating depression, they could be pardoned. But there's no sign of this. Surrounded by neighbors, many of them English-speakers who could communicate their sympathy best with silence, they buried Tjark on a rise of land not far from present-day Golden, Illinois. There was no priest or pastor to say the words, no comforting liturgy to ease the passing, no familiar foods or smells to comfort the living.

How did the survivors deal with their losses? Perhaps in the dark of night tears soaked their pillows—tears for the dead, tears of self-pity for their terrible misfortunes—that's if exhaustion from pain or the day's toil left them with the energy to cry. Yet through this, they clearly recognized a home truth—they needed more of their own folk around them to lighten the load of labor, to ease them in times of grief, and to create here on this fertile prairie a replica of the culture that had allowed them to survive in the hostile fens along the North Sea.

They'd had misfortune, yes, and were in a precarious situation. Also true. Why? Because there weren't enough of them. But if they could survive this first year and persuade more of their folk to come and settle the prairie around them, they would build a hedge against the future and could then deal with disaster the way their forbearers had—by working, praying and playing together. Thus, Jann's letters home were full of the wonders of this new land.

There was much to marvel about and aspects to be glossed over. Like the heat and humidity. The days just kept getting hotter as what was left of the two families struggled into August trying to cope with the debilitating sun and the sweltering humidity. Even the approach to New Orleans through the Mississippi delta hadn't affected them so dearly. But they had no choice. "As you begin, so you will go on," was an aphorism that guided their days. They did what they had to do. They kept moving, kept working, kept trying.

In the first days, Ickka and Gesche would have established their new-world work routines—ones devised to keep the children safe and fed while allowing time to do the myriad of other chores like caring for Jann, the baby, and the animals they'd bought, while working through their lists of "things that needed doing before winter." What they certainly did not do? They didn't tackle the swampy virgin prairie soil.

We don't know quite when the sod-busting began, but probably not until late July or early August when one or more of the neighbors could spare their oxen to pull the deep plows required to do the job.

What a grand day, what a boost to everyone's spirits, when someone shouted, "They're coming. I hear them. I hear them."

One of the family would have run to swing their Ostfriesen gate wide on its pivot and to welcome the teams that came accompanied by a low rumble, like that of kettle drums. In fact the noise of the oxen passing would have been music to everyone's ears--the jangle of harness, the calls of the drivers, the squeaking and groaning of wheels, all as harmonious as the instruments in a symphonic orchestra. And so the plows arrived at the Buss homestead, emerging from the prairie as if conjured by the very earth that trembled under hooves and wheels.

"They're here."

The massive oxen, eight to a plow, bent under their heavy yokes, and drew their burdens through the Friesen gate where young Gerd might have been standing on the pivot, staring at ploughshares that to his eyes would have seemed as big as houses and as sharp and shiny as a row of swords. They were weapons of death, and no one could mistake them for anything else.

Well. Of course. It wasn't easy to kill a section of virgin prairie, but these machines could do the job. Here were man-made, massive claws designed to rip the heart out of the land and spread its still beating flesh out to bake in the sun.

Ickka, though, would've had no such thoughts. She probably saw this day as another beginning, as the moment when she and Jann could launch the serious work of farming their new land. But it was more.

Ickka and Jann had bought one of the last bits of raw Illinois prairie and "busting" it was a scene in the last act in a long drama—one that had been bloody, lacking in romance, and ugly.

On this day, long whips cracked, oxen strained, wheels turned, and sharp blades descended to slash through dense patterns of grasses and roots, clawing down and into the subsoil. Exposed layers rolled upwards.

There was no warning for the world far below the prairie's surface, only the trembling of land under the oxen's hooves as the big beasts strained through belly-deep grass thick with flowers and bugs and over a subterranean system sheltering burrows eras old. Great brown oxen eyes blinked against the swarms of insects—mites, mosquitoes, flies, bees, butterflies, moths—that swarmed upwards shrouding the teams in brown, dense clouds. Veterans of this phenomenon, the ploughmen lowered veils from their hats and, thus protected, kept the teams moving, their long whips cracking. "Gee up, Spot. Hut, Boy."

Behind them they left black and muddy exposed earth rolled back and curled onto itself the way a piece of paper thrown on a fire bends backwards as its edges singe. Rabbits screamed and shot sideways away from one blade and into another. Snakes were severed into pieces. Ground owls flapped to gain altitude, desperately and vainly seeking air to lift their wings as descending rolls of black dirt drove them back under the plow. Badgers, shrews, prairie dogs, foxes, moles fled. A centuries-old ecosystem was being destroyed. It did not die peacefully or quietly.

To Ickka and Jann this carnage was a bonus; the occasion joyous. Spread before them was not only the beginning of tame farmland but a bounty of meat. Iccka probably waded in to bang the remaining life out of injured rabbits and weasels, ground squirrels and prairie dogs and to toss their carcasses onto a sheet or apron to drag away. Here was proof of the land's beneficence. If only they could collect and preserve all of it. An impossibility, of course. But what they couldn't save for the dinner table would rejoin with and enrich the soil.

And so the first of the Buss family fields provided an unexpected but welcome bounty.

As for Ickka and Gesche's garden, almost miraculously to northern European eyes, it began to produce an abundance that far exceeded expectations. While they couldn't keep up with the weeds, which grew back faster than they could hoe them, it didn't seem to matter. Even with knee-high volunteers choking the garden, the cabbages were huge, the potatoes thick and long, the onions fat.

Jann recovered. He worked from dawn to dark in this strange land, probably telling himself that here he was a rich man. He wrote home to encourage others to follow him. He had an impossible amount of land, acreage the nobility at home would envy. He had a rifle he could use in more than just target shooting. He could leave at breakfast and stalk his own land to bag a deer. Had he ever dreamed so big as to imagine owning a private hunting reserve?

"Damn few," he might have muttered as he decapitated a snake with his hoe, wiped mud from his hands, or erected a scarecrow to frighten away the swarms of birds that threatened to eat his grain before it even ripened.

But what about quality of life?

Jann no doubt had his frustrations which he would have kept to himself or, at most, shared with his brother-in-law. Here he was in a foreign place, put at a disadvantage by the language barrier and by a poor understanding of the laws and customs.

Added to this was mortification and a likely sense of humiliation. The bee accident had revealed him to the community not as a man among men but as a bumbling peasant who'd been laid low by a swarm of bees. Ten-year-old American boys could drive a team of horses, but he'd shown he couldn't. And to be knocked off his feet by something as ridiculous as a insect bites? To be the subject of scorn because of a bug the size of his little fingernail?

It was a fact. Jann had traded in a skill at which he excelled— sailing canal barges—and the admiration of business colleagues, customers, and neighbors. In exchange he had the unremitting, heat-stroke inducing drudgery of farming. He'd abandoned days skimming the canals, waving at the pretty girls, gossiping with the women at his stops, exchanging political news with men who listened to him and looked up to him. And what did he get? Endless, back-breaking toil under a sun so hot he could feel his flesh cooking.

No more would he stop for a pint at days end, knowing every man in the pub … actually related in one way or another to all of them. No more would he loiter alongside a pier to watch a great ship come in from the Orient carrying slant-eyed men.

Never again would he look into shops heaped with exotic wares, exuding strange smells.

Instead, when the light faded, he'd walk into a mean log hut with a dirt floor where sniveling, dirty brats looked at him with wide eyes and where a red-faced woman—her sweat-wet hair stringing from under her cap—ladled porridge and meat from a pot hung over a fire. At least there was beer. And Jann might well have sat in the doorway of a late evening, drinking a home brew, and brooding.

That was one side of the Buss family life.

On the other, they would have had a cow to supply milk, and she would have done well on the prairie grass. Their heifers no doubt matured, and Ickka most likely walked them as far as was necessary to be serviced by a neighbor's bull. They'd probably bought a bred sow which would have harrowed, producing a passel of squirming piglets. This would have seemed a miracle of sort—the first births in their new land, the first truly auspicious sign that their luck had turned.

Also, two more Ostfriesen families arrived, and this had an immediate effect on morale. South Prairie began to feel a bit like home. More, all of a sudden Jann and Gerd were the old-timers, the experts, the go-to men. That part was all very satisfactory.

Before that first winter set in, therefore, and despite the back-breaking labor and skin chafed by rashes and bug-bites, and never mind the snakes and wild animals, Ickka and Jann probably felt, in various degrees, that they had done what was needed. Their surviving children were brown and healthy. They had assembled a snug if cramped home, had a fireplace and hearth to keep them warm. They had planted and harvested a truck garden and a crop and had sufficient food preserved and stored to see themselves and their livestock through the winter.

Winter came, and Ickka most likely expected it to be more to her liking than the misery of the summer heat. She was accustomed to moaning, freezing winds, stinging sleet and snow, and harsh winters. Illinois winters, everyone said, had a lot in common with her homeland. Bone cold is bone cold. Surely, the woolens that had tortured them over the summer would prove their worth now.

Yet, Illinois surprised with deep snow, solid ice, and blizzards so fierce a man could be lost only feet from his own door. Caring for livestock was agony. Frostbite was a constant danger as buckets of water had to be pulled from the well and given to the livestock immediately or the iced-over bucket brought in the house to sit by the fire. Animals left to forage for themselves broke through ice on the creek and died or just died from exposure.

And, there were none of the simple amenities Ickka'd taken for granted in Ludwigsdorf—no source for supplies closer than Quincy, no schools for her children, no doctors to mend broken bones, and only itinerant ministers of other denominations for spiritual comfort.

But they survived. They learned. They helped each other where required. They gathered for Sunday prayers as often as they could. The women taught their children their letters. As more of their near and distantly related kin arrived, they raised barns, fenced fields, and erected houses with stout walls. Lutheran preachers eventually found them, married their children, and said words over their dead. Churches, schools, and communities formed.

In a matter of a few short years, Ickka could look around at the many Ostfriesen families surrounding her and feel at home. South Prairie had become a New Ostfriesland. As expected, the rest of Jann's siblings (except Tette Christina) made the move with their families, most choosing the easy route through New Orleans and up the river, one coming the harder way via New York, which meant dealing with the expense and complexities of overland travel.

Another of the Franken men, a blacksmith, arrived and set up shop. The people placed a blockhouse near him to serve as a church, one they called the Immanuel Lutheran Church of South Prairie and, just like that, the South Prairie immigrants had a community center. Eventually, more than 350 East Friesen families would settle in the 44 square mile area around the Buss and Franken home farms providing the support and communality the first families had so craved that first summer.

As for Ickka, her experiences had changed her beyond all recognition. The female chattel, the "laborer" who had left Bremerhaven, had learned from this new land. She had worked alongside her husband. She had taken charge when he could not. She had exercised her imagination and her brain. Perhaps best of all, she had status in her community not just as a wife but both as a pioneer and as a woman widely admired, a role model, a person to be emulated.

If someone had asked her about this, she would have looked at the questioner with her hawk-like eyes and said, "How not?"

As the days turned into months and the seasons followed each other around and around, Ickka's life settled into a routine similar to the one in Ludwigsdorf. Pregnant or not, she hauled water, fed and doctored animals, preserved food, prepared meals, washed up, built fires, chopped wood, made and mended clothing, and … who else would watch the children? They had to be kept from edging too close to fires or tumbling into the nearby creek. They had to learn which snakes were dangerous, taught to do simple chores, and, above all, made to understand they should never wander far from their parents or the cabin. The infants as they came had to be nursed, burped, and changed, nappies washed, bottoms kept free of rash. It was almost like home.

The new world, though, had down sides for Ickka, too. She was a nursing mother again and again to four more babies, sweating in her long-skirted, high-necked dresses, often lacking the fresh produce her body needed to nourish her young, skating always on the edge of dehydration. Her skin would have burned from the Illinois sun, so different from the pale yellow orb that shone on the North Sea lands. Bugs would have added to her miseries, swarms of mosquitoes descending at night, leaving the exposed areas of her body covered in welts. During the day it would have been flies, dominated by the painful bites of deer flies. Up and busy at dawn, Ickka would still have been working when the last light faded from the western sky, endlessly exhausted, maybe worried about Jann, maybe bruised as collateral damage to Jann's frustration and feelings of loss. Above all, Ickka constantly feared for the safety of her little ones.

Their most immediate danger came from snakes. Poisonous snakes. Pioneering diaries, journals, and letters were larded with stories about them. They were bad in summer but worse in winter when the warmth of fires brought them out of their nests in and under the logs of the houses. Tales about women and children seeking safety atop tables and chairs made for laughter but were far from funny for those involved. Nor was it pleasant to wake up with a rattlesnake nestled in your blankets as a sleeping partner. Snake bites were common as were broken bones, dysentery, colds and flus. A catalog of other diseases and ailments explains why the opium-laced tonics sold by itinerant medicine hawkers were so popular. If you couldn't cure it, you could at least blunt the worry and pain.

Yet the land was rich. Nothing said about it had been exaggerated. Once the ground was properly prepared, all you had to do was drop a seed to have it spring up and grow and grow and grow. Surely the tale of Jack and the Beanstalk came from new settlers on the prairie marveling at just how high a plant could climb.

Because of this, there would have come a day when Ickka and Jann's exhaustion fell away with the sheer wonder of the abundance of it all. Given their stoic upbringings, it's unlikely they danced or sang or joined hands and capered about with joy. There would have been only an extra prayer in the religious services on Sundays. It was worth it, after all.

There was a positive side to the wildlife, too. No one who owned a rifle and was a reasonable shot could go hungry for long. As he had probably fantasized, Jann Buss learned to hunt. Jann's first deer kill in America would have been a red-letter occasion. That night as Ickka roasted a haunch over the fire would have been a time for remembering stories about Ickka's grandfather, Eiler Aljets—famous for having shot a stag that had developed a taste for his crops. Probably chuckling, Jann would have related the story to his children, and young Gerd Buss would have listened in awe to how his great grandfather had killed the big buck.

He probably heard about what a great shot his great grandfather had been and learned about the famous *schützenfests* or shooting festivals of Ostfriesland where the best shot among the men would be crowed the *schützenkönig*, taking home the year's trophy. His maternal great grandfather might even have been a king of shooters!

But if Eiler Aljets had been such a great shot, why couldn't he hunt? Why would he be punished for shooting a deer?

These were questions Jann would've had to answer after he finished the story, perhaps saying, "So what did old Eiler do? Why he loaded some cheese and bread into a pack and set out for Berlin to see the king. He hiked all the long way, and Frederick the Great was so impressed by Eiler Aljets that he gave him absolution." That was the way the family story went.

True? Probably not the part about the hike to Berlin. Ostfriesland was then, by treaty, a province of Prussia and nominally under Frederick who was King of Prussia. That part was right enough. But the province was actually autonomous and ruled by a famous Friesen chancellor, Sebastian Homfeld, a Rheiderlander prince, who rumor says had poisoned the last Ostfriesen prince in order to supplant him. Of course, there might be an even more interesting story here if Eiler had reason to go over Homfeld's head to Frederick and if Frederick chose to insult the chancellor by honoring Eiler's request.

Makes one wonder. Whatever. Jann's first deer kill would have been a wonderful event, underscoring the bounty of this great new country. His family would not starve to death here, that much was clear. But as the events of these past months had shown, the land had dozens of other ways of killing them.

PART TWO
THE MÜLLERS OF BÜHREN

The mill at Bühren. Evergreen wrapped gate declares the owner is the
district champion marksman, the king of shooters.
Photo compliments of Minna and Tina Meinen.

The Müllers of Bühren Family Tree

Harmen Janssen Müller   Conrad Hansen

Jancken Harmen (? – 1684)   m. 1676   Hans Conrads (1650-1699)

Weyert Conrads Müller (1707-1795) m. Hiske Gerdes (1713-1790)

Gerd Hanken Weyerts (1737-1794) m. 1767 Gebke Weyen (1747-1770)

Eilert Gerdes Müller (1789-1858) m. 1810 Thaete Leena Focken (1787-1814)

| Gerd Hanken (1813-1881)
| Gerdje Eilerts (1811-1827)

m. 1815 Moder Heeren Wallrich (1794-1847)

| Thete Lena (1816-?)
| Herman Eilerts (1817-1876) m. 1841 Behrendji Berends de Groot (1809-98)
Conrad Eilerts (1820-1822)
Johann Hinrichs (1822- ?)
Wallrich (1857-1886)
Gerhard (1830 - ?)

m. 1850 Anna Jurgens Wilkens (1823-1891)

| Gerdje   Moder   Antje   Ellerdina

12
The Müllers of Bühren, 1846

The Ostfriesen Müllers who would intermarry with Ickka's children were from a hamlet named Bühren, a thirty-minute stroll from the village of Remels in the district of Uplengen. Their land was … well, land. It was wet, yes, but it was slightly higher and drained much more easily than the countryside twenty miles to the north and west where Jann Buss plied his trade. Storms blowing in off the North Sea blanketed Bühren with heavy fogs and rains no better or worse than elsewhere, but for the most part incursions of sea water and the swampy fen conditions prevailing in much of Ostfriesland were notable for their absence.

Most important, economically, there were no peat bogs and, for the most part, roads rather than canals carried produce and travelers. It was partly thanks to the latter fact that the Müllers prospered. Their home did duty as an inn/restaurant/pub/shop/stable. In twenty-first century terms, it was an I-95 or U-Bahn service plaza. Just like these, the Bühren Mill House sat on a good road, the Bührener Strasse near an intersection with one of Uplengen's main arteries—the L24 or the GrossSander Strasse. But the main source of Müller income was, as their name suggests, milling grains.

Possession of a mill put the family in the highest of the Hannoverian-designated economic brackets. They were considered rich, which had everything to do with their ability to pay taxes and quarter and feed troops and very little to do with social status. All that said, their quality of life was far from enviable by today's standards. While the Müllers had a guaranteed source of income, their work was back-breaking and sometimes dangerous. As for a miller's actual place in the community … well … to the government he was a cash cow, his fellow merchants viewed him as an opportunist, and the farmers who relied on his services routinely suspected him of cheating on weights. Good, bad or indifferent, though, the Müllers perched on the opposite end of the economic ladder from Ickka Eilert's father, Gerd, while sharing with him the same stubborn approach to life, the same independent spirit, pride, and work ethic.

Proprietorship of the mill was a mixed blessing for the Müllers. It gave them their primary source of income, but it also ruled their lives and tied them to a piece of property. This particular mill had been built sometime in the 1600's and was owned by the (now) St. Martens Lutheran Church in Remels. It seems to have come to our particular müllers through marriage in about 1684 when a thirty-four year old Ostfriesen named Hans Conrads married Janken Harmens, the daughter of Harmen Janssen Müller. Thereafter, the descendants of Hans Conrads and Janken Harmens adopted Janken's last name and held the lease onward as an ensured tenancy—meaning that as long as the Müllers met their tenant obligations, the mill was theirs in perpetuity.

Tenancies and ensured tenancies were an essential element of the medieval system, the brainchild of some early Machiavelli and the rope with which men were permanently tied to the land, thus becoming serfs—essentially slaves. Elsewhere in Europe this economic agrarian model guaranteed a caste system. Among the Ostfriesens, not so much, although a form of tenancy was alive and well and living in Bühren in the shape of its mill.

The Müller family might have the right to run the mill, but as a matter of fact if not law the mill owned them, not vice versa. Unlike serfs, they could leave. As a practical matter, though, they couldn't. Not without abandoning their livelihood and the generations of investments and improvements they'd made to the property, all of which would revert to the church should they fail to meet their obligations.

Despite its age, the Bühren mill, a sturdy structure built with massive wooden beams and thick wood planks, was a well-maintained building that had aged to iron. There, wagons would line up during harvests to unload their bags of wheat or buckwheat or rye while other wagons sat ready to haul off the milled grain. Rain or sunshine, horses waited patiently in harness as the millers worked and the drivers stood about gossiping or talking politics. Those that could afford a drink or a meal would walk next door and through the door of the Mill House to sample what the Müller women could provide in the way of food or ale or to browse through their shelves of merchandise and possibly buy a ribbon for the daughter or wife. And, for those who'd come from afar or were just passing—the tinkers and traders, the post and the travelers? There was always a meal and bed, stabling for horses or a basin of hot water for sore feet.

Thus it might have continued to the present, albeit with the three hundred-year-old mill converted to a twenty-first century photo op. That is, it might have if not for an American B-29 Superfortress bomber.

One day in 1944 a young American, perhaps of German or Ostfriesen descent, looked down through his sights and saw not an industrial complex but a picture-perfect, quaint smock mill of the type painted on Dutch china, one with cloth sails, a rotating cap, and four inside levels holding massive grinding stones—all covered with a flaring outer surface in the shape of a smock. Hence, the label "smock mill." He didn't know it, but this antique was still attached to the Müller family, cousins of third- and fourth-generation American Millers.

Was he bored with flattening cities and shipyards? Had he run out of targets? Or was he mentally playing a game of "let's see if I can hit that?" Or, perhaps, the mill was actually on a list of targets selected for destruction as a way of breaking civilian morale. Leaving aside the reason, this young man lined up his sights and hit the mill, destroying the centuries-old structure, removing an historic relic before—overtaken by new technologies as it had been—it could become just another tourist destination, another page in a picture book, another window into the past. But that was all a hundred years in the future.

The part of the story that would concern Ickka Eilerts Buss began in the 1840's with a strongly built man of late middle age with a long face and a high forehead emphasized by a receding hair line. He had blue eyes that focused widely, taking in not just what was immediately in front of him but what had been and could come. At the same time, his was a pleasant expression—a good face for a shop and innkeeper. He was a man you instinctively wanted to know.

His name was Eilert Gerdes Müller, the great great grandson of Hans Conrads and Jancken Harmens. He was the Bühren miller and a man of parts, a leader in his community, a skilled marksman—a repeated holder of the honored title *schützenkönig* (champion marksman)—and a crafty businessman. Under his father's hands the mill and its affiliated businesses had prospered enough to support eleven children. Eilert Gerdes aimed to do better. While he hadn't yet sired as many offspring as his father, he'd already buried one wife who'd borne him two children, had remarried, and had another six.

Even with all these mouths to feed and after subtracting upkeep, rents, and taxes, he still managed a steady expansion of his land holdings. Thus, by the mid-1840's, he was sufficiently well off that he could deed over a farm and house to his oldest son, Gerd Hanken, who was his only surviving child by his first wife. Gerd had married in 1838 and apparently had little interest in the mill or its various associated enterprises. Instead, he farmed with his wife and their three children, a fourth being born in that famine year of 1848.

The center of Eilert Gerdes' life, the Mill House, was an expansive structure of two stories which had been built by his father, Gerd Hanken, in the mid-1700's. It sat directly alongside the high road so that passers-by couldn't miss it, the mill looming just behind, a capacious yard joining the two with the mill's associated sheds and providing ample space for wagons, horses, carriages, and carts to maneuver.

Customers for the Mill House walked directly into a great room equipped with trestle tables, a fireplace, a corner with goods for sale, and a food preparation and cooking area. There were a few chairs with backs, but most diners/drinkers sat on stools or benches near the fire. Behind this room, one can imagine the family's common area with its own stove for heat and stools where the men sat in the evening and where the women carded and spun yarn, quilted and worked a loom, prepared and cooked food for family and guests.

Further back, an aisle of straight stalls with brick flooring provided stabling for guests' and family horses. The wall of the aisle was set with hooks and racks to hold harness and other livery items, the stalls equipped with mangers. Next came pens for other animals and, finally, a covered area for fine equipages and farm equipment. Above this on the second floor was a spacious loft. One end served as a hay store. The other contained guest rooms with beds of different quality—all meant to be shared when necessary. In the middle were bedrooms for family members.

When the great famine of 1846 spread across Europe, the big house held eight adults and two children. At home, of course, was Eilert Gerdes and his second wife, Moder Wallrich, their oldest daughter Theete Lena, plus four sons, one daughter-in-law, and two granddaughters. Moder ruled the mill household with Theete Lena and the oldest son's wife, Behrendje Berends, doing as told. It's likely that Moder also had a village girl or two to help with the serving and cleaning and a boy to tend guests' horses as well as to run errands, clean tack, and do odd jobs. And, as we'll see later, it's probable that Behrendje Berends brought a serving girl (an illegitimate niece named Anna Berends) with her when she married into the family.

As the master of this establishment, Eilert Gerdes played a supervisory role, directing his four younger sons, consigning the heavy labor to them. After fifty-odd years, he was an old man by eighteenth century standards and most likely left the hard work of ratcheting around the mill's cap (to move the sails into the wind) and the harvest-time tasks of changing the massive millstones (to match the type of stone to the grain being ground) to the younger generation. Certainly, he'd long since stopped hauling sacks of grain up to the stones. Of a morning, therefore, he would map out the day's work among his sons and then would spend the hours until dark touring his holdings to plan out the next set of jobs.

At 29, Hermann Müller was the oldest of the sons at home and Behrendje's husband. Since his older half-brother, Gerd, had left the mill to become a farmer, Hermann would inherit the tenancy and was already master of the mill in all but name. During harvest periods, he would be joined in the mill by his brothers, the four of them efficiently keeping the grain flowing, watching the weights, and collecting cash or kind for their labor. In other seasons his work revolved around mill maintenance.

The next oldest son, Johann Hinrichs, was 24 and as yet unmarried. Like Gerd, who had given up his rights to the mill in favor of farming, Johann had distanced himself from the family's various enterprises. He presumably did farm work although that isn't clear, and he may have eventually become one of an army of younger sons who set out on a back-breaking quest to win their own land from the moors.

Nineteen-year-old Wallrich was a different story. They say he had a real flare for business and was already handling the restaurant, pub, inn, and the little retail area. Later in life he became quite a successful merchant. But in 1846?

There's no doubt that the women did the actual day-to-day work inside the Mill House, deciding on the daily menu, brewing the beer, crafting objects for sale, making beds, cleaning rooms, and building fires. They processed, preserved, stored and cooked food. They worked piles of fleece into blankets and clothing. They chopped the heads off chickens, geese, and ducks, plucked them, preserved the down and made mattresses and pillows. They did all of this as well as handling the myriad of other chores connected to the family's survival and its profit margin. As the master's wife, we can be certain that Moder was dead center in the daily flurry, managing everything, directing the other women, her hands busy from dawn to dusk.

No man did women's work. So what was left for young Wallrich? He likely would have been set to minding the cash register, it being less likely that a "guest" would try to leave without paying if a strong young man was there to collect from him. Wallrich may have done the books, as well, and he certainly would've learned how to cost out the Mill House offerings.

How much did the baby of the family, Gerhard Eylerts, contribute to this? He was just 16 but was more than capable of doing a man's work. In all probability he was set to whatever task needed an extra pair of hands.

However the work was divided, it got done, and as 1846 opened the Müllers combination of interstate/autobahn service plaza-type businesses was thriving.

That changed. The famine, drought, and economic collapse of 1846 rolled into the Uplengen district by degrees. As movement in the nearby ports and on the canals and roads slowed and news from elsewhere on the continent became grimmer and ever worse, the people of Uplengen tightened their belts. Farmers cut back on their tilled acreage, focused on growing food for their own survival, shied away from raising cash crops, and milled only that needed for their own tables. Men hoarded what money they had, and those capable of paying travelled only when absolutely necessary. Gradually, business fell away. Everywhere.

The word 'globilization' had yet to be coined and what happened next was hardly on a global scale, but already economic developments in one part of Europe affected everyone else. Lacking instantaneous communications and social media, the process took longer but was inevitable. As we saw when looking at what happened to Jann Buss's business, the collapse of the peat market and shipping shut Ostfriesland down, drove the people back to a subsistence level.

God knows, there were still people on the roads. But they weren't the same type of people. Increasingly, business travelers on horseback and traders with their carts were replaced by out-of-work single men with packs hiking to who-knows-where … anywhere offering work. In time, these solitary men were augmented by the tramping feet of entire families with worldly possessions stacked on hand carts or on their backs. For the most part, the families knew where they were going, were hoping to find shelter with better-off relatives, expected that by working together they might all survive as a unit. Some, too, were already on their way to America, headed for Bremen or its almost new port of Bremerhaven.

This internal migration brought little business to the Mill House doors. The travelers didn't stop except, as things grew worse, they would camp by the mill. If they had money, they hoarded it, reluctant to pay for a roof or a meal or even a fire. No surprise, the odd chicken disappeared. A sow might lose a piglet. A cow could come in from pasture drained of milk. Ostfriesens weren't thieves, but when a man or his children are starving? The rules of law tend to be suspended while moral values changed.

Other things happened in these impromptu camps. Bad things. Harmful things. Women sold their bodies. Women and girls were raped. Men gambled and drank themselves to a stupor. Youngsters became thieves. Babies died.

All this happened outside the Mill House doors, and who could turn a blind eye to such human misery? Moder, Theete and Behrendje could do little and would no doubt have grumbled, but they also would've seen to it that no child continued up the road without a bowl of warm gruel in his belly.

There was an uptick in violence, along with the rest. Tempers ran close to the surface. Men tended to take the law into their own hands when confronted with an injustice. Worse, men with hungry-eyed, hollow-cheeked children couldn't weep but could rage and strike out at the nearest person, usually a smaller and weaker family member. Or a woman without a cup of buckwheat left to boil would see her man returning with the smell of beer on his breath. She couldn't retrieve the money he'd spent, but she could take a broom handle to him.

The Bühren Müllers themselves would not starve nor would they suffer greatly. Their problems were minor compared to the needs of the many. Their cash income might be meager, but as long as they could pay their taxes and church rent, they and their livestock would have a roof over their heads and could feed themselves off their farm holdings. They may have complained when their favorite consumables disappeared, but they wouldn't have done so loudly enough to be overheard. They were lucky and they knew it. Tea, cotton cloth for shirts and dresses, sugar—these and other items bought and sold and used by them as a matter of course in 1845 became items that gathered dust on their shelves. Good salt became scarce, opiates used in medications disappeared, pipe tobacco cost a fortune.

Other things changed, too. Some grain still needed milling for home consumption, but farmers wanted to pay in kind rather than cash. Some few thaler-carrying travelers still arrived at the Mill House doors and were duly housed and fed, copiously if plainly, while those camping in the yard ate of the leftovers. Of an evening, Bühren and Remels men desperate for company would gather at the trestle tables in the big front room but would buy nothing or would nurse one mug of beer until closing.

Newspapers—long a staple of the Mill House—became a luxury and those left behind by travelers were passed from hand to hand and read until every bit of news had been memorized. Even then they weren't thrown away or burned but were recycled and became wall insulation or formed mats to sleep on or were stuffed into overlarge boots and shoes or found dozens of other uses. Newspapers were not unique, of course, in that sense. No object was discarded easily or for long.

The Müller men devoted more time to their animals and their land and to guarding both from destructive thieving. The work of the Müller women was reduced only in terms of quantities and types of food prepared. Otherwise the ladies barely noticed the change in their fortunes.

As did everyone, the family expected a turn-around in 1847. As with everyone, they didn't get it. "It's got to be a better year," they said.

It wasn't.

Instead, Moder Wallrich Müller died, leaving a large gap in the household, particularly on the distaff side, one that would have a ripple effect with many repercussions. Remove a keystone from an arch, and it'll collapse but perhaps not immediately. The adjacent stones might lean in and support each other for a time—not long, but a time—and so it happened here.

As the daughter of the house, Theete Lena had a moral right to take over her mother's keys. She was no longer a girl, was thirty-one years old and knew every inch of the house and its affairs. She was strong and capable with a proven track record in all the necessary skills. But would her even older and much more experienced sister-in-law tolerate this?

Behrendje had come into the Müller family as a widow. She'd had her own household during her previous marriage and, after that, had run her own affairs for two years. Even so, she'd allowed herself to be kept under Moder's thumb for six additional years which could be said to be more than an adequate period of apprenticeship. Would she now let Theete Lena boss her around?

Not likely. They were two proud, experienced, and capable women with only one management position available. Could the job be divided? Were there other potential solutions? One had to be found for the immediate sake of domestic tranquillity. Just as importantly, if not more so, the solution might determine the pecking order among the Müller men and the future of the family.

Whether anyone said a word or not, the issue was clear. It may not have actually divided the men, but it brought them to the table with different frames of reference. Theete's father and most of her brothers, of course, had to support tradition—the oldest adult daughter in the house succeeded the mother unless and until the father remarried. Hermann would've offered a codicil to that, saying "Or unless there are compelling reasons for a different woman to take charge." Because Hermann was in an awkward position. Either he supported his wife or faced a cold shoulder and a cold bed. More, he had a vested interest in her ascendancy.

Here was a story as old as the human race, one with a compelling plot and an equally interesting sub-plot. Because this wasn't just about household management and a passive use of female power. Because like it or not, here was an issue where the young buck could challenge the older without recourse to strength or moral authority. Here, wrapped up in a domestic dress, was a challenge to the old man. If Behrendje became mistress of the Mill House, her husband would inevitably be seen by the community as its master. No doubt he was already doing most of Eilert Gerdes' work. It would be a 'de facto' changing of the guard. Like it or not Eilert Gerdes would gradually be consigned to a chair by the fire.

The outcome? In a surprise move, Theete Lena left the battlefield. She married.

Who arranged it? At thirty-one, Theete Lena was an old maid by anyone's standards and about as likely to find a man for her bed as an exposed worm was to escape a robin. Why she, the daughter of a prosperous man of Uplengen, would have remained unmarried so long is anyone's guess but there are three possibilities as to why and how she married now: she gussied herself up and went hunting; Eilert Gerdes upped the size of her dowry; or Hermann offered to augment an existing dowry.

Of the three scenarios, the second is the most likely. But however it was done, Theete Lena's removal from the scene defused the situation. Behrendje became chatelaine by default not by merit or because she was Hermann's wife. Eilert Gerdes' prestige and standing with his sons and in the community was left unchanged. He had ceded nothing. Hermann had won nothing.

As for Behrendje, she now had the keys to their little kingdom, but it was a Pyrrhic victory. When Theete Lena said, "I do," to her new spouse, Heinrich Friedrich Meyer, in 1848 and waved goodbye from the flower-bedecked carriage that took her to her new home, she left Behrendje behind not just as chatelaine but as the sole caretaker of the Mill House. The work that three women had barely had time or energy to accomplish was hers alone. Even with servants to help, she had a large building, five adult males and her two little girls, travelers, customers, and a long list of animals to tend. Plus she was pregnant again.

13
Behrendji

Behrendji's early life is something of a mystery. Born the daughter of a *colonist* of Schwerinsdorf and the granddaughter of a *heuerman* (someone who rents his land rather than owns it) in Stiekelkamperfehn, some ten miles from Bühren, Behrendje Behrends De Groot (alternate spelling, De Groth) came into the world the year her father, Berend De Groot, died. He was only 42 years-old, but had been married eighteen years before leaving his 42-year-old wife, Tabea Schroder, with a newborn and an unknown number of other children. We can safely assume that after so much time and with Tabea still obviously fertile that there'd been more than a few of them. At the average Ostfriesen rate of one every two years, an educated guess would give baby Behrendji some seven older siblings.

Among these, possibly, was one Antje Berends De Groot—and we'll hear more about her later.

In the meantime, how did the mother of all these children manage? The family histories don't say. It's unlikely that Berend left her well provided. As a *colonist,* one who reclaimed land, he had title to at least a small plot of land and owned a house—likely one that looked much the same as Ickka's childhood home. That said, Tabea would not have inherited but would've seen such property deeded to one of her sons. The idea of such practice was for the son to then look after the mother.

Yet, in this case the oldest child would have been seventeen at the most and could've well been a girl. What then?

There were a number of other options. Tabea might have remarried. One of her husband's male relatives might've stepped in, providing her with a small living in exchange for use of the land. Or the family might've been dispersed among various relatives—Tabea going into service for a wealthier family.

In these circumstances, we'd expect Behrendji to marry at a fairly early age, particularly since she was a pretty girl with delicate features. She did not. But what she did do through her teens and into her twenties is unknown.

However she managed, she survived and flourished, among other things learning to play the piano. That latter fact would seem to be a clue since the homes of *colonists* were not known as venues for pianos. Instead, it simply adds to the mystery and invites all sorts of speculation.

 Eventually, when she was 23, she married a thirty-one-year-old *chaussie* from the nearby town of Hesel named Christoph Focken Buecker or Becker. What kind of life did she have? Judging by the fact that Behrendji went to her next marriage with a number of pieces of very fine furniture, she was relatively well off. With the additional clue that she eventually named a son after her first husband, we can assume Christoph Becker was a good man who treated her well.

His profession as given on his wedding certificate, *chaussie,* translates as "driver" or "carter."

What does this mean? In Ostfriesland in those years, he could have been employed to drive a cart, wagon or carriage for some wealthy person or he could have owned his horse and wagon and been a land road equivalent of Jann Buss with his canal boat, taking goods from towns and cities to consumers in the countryside. Finally, the 'carter' profession also refers to a man who owns a haulage business, moving larger cargos on heavy drays pulled by teams of horses, plying the roads between the port cities of Hannover and their customers in Ostfriesland.

Of these various possibilities, it's likely that Christoph had a modest business—substantial enough to provide Behrendji with her carved, black walnut furniture and a suitable house to hold it. Christoph, himself, would have been away from home a good deal, just as Jann Buss was.

Unlike Ickka Buss, though, Behrendji may well have learned to help her husband's business affairs by organizing his cargo, keeping his books, and directing the daily running of his yard, stables, and storage houses. In all of this, she would've had help: a maid or two in the house and, most particularly, a scullery maid in the kitchen. Outside, there would be a boy/man or two to mind the animals and keep the yard.

So, her days would have been full, but with time left over to drink tea with the wives of other villagers, to organize church activities, and to be part of a community of women.

Yet, year after year went by and she bore no live children— whether there were stillborn or natural abortions we don't know. In this male-dominant society where children were valued almost higher than the coin of the realm, where premarital sex was permissible as a way of ensuring a man did not marry an empty womb, childlessness was a stigma. A woman so afflicted, no matter how pretty or talented, how accomplished or intelligent, lacked value. She had failed at her highest purpose. If her body didn't produce an infant every two years, she was taking up space and resources a fertile woman could better fill.

How Behrendji felt about it while Christoph still lived was one thing, but he died seven years into the marriage. Thereafter, she not only slept in a lonely bed but lived in a silent house. She was still young, but who would marry her now? She must've faced this unpalatable fact during her period of mourning as she prayed under the vaulted roof of her church every Sunday morning and looked across the aisle at the available bachelors. The first year went by—no problem. It would've been unseemly to remarry too fast. Or so she might have consoled herself. The second year, though, was another matter.

Had she met Hermann Müller previously? As a carter, Christoph moved around the countryside and almost certainly knew the Müllers of Bühren, a village only six miles distant from Hesel. He could well have hauled milled grain from there into Uplengen or even as far as Aurich, staying at the millhouse while his drays were loaded and bringing home stories of the Müller family.

No matter how Hermann and Behrendji met, there's the real question of why Hermann would be interested in a childless, older widow no matter how attractive. He was in line to inherit the Bühren mill tenancy and would be an excellent match for any woman. He was also a fine-looking figure of a man—tall, strong, and … young. His face was a bit long to be considered handsome, but his features were regular, put together in a pleasing fashion, and his eyes revealed an inner gentleness. Also, like his father, he was a *schützenkönig*—a man above men. As they say, "he could have his pick."

Certainly, the girls of Remels and the adjoining larger town of Uplengen, would've considered him a catch, would've looked sideways at him from under their bonnets and the lace on their snoods. On festival days there would have been half a dozen pretty things throwing themselves in his direction, perhaps even proposing. On any Sunday of the year, there were flirtatious glances from the female side of the church, and mothers angling for a chance to take him home for dinner.

Behrendje wasn't one of them. She went to church a few miles away in Hesel. Besides, he was only 24. She was a matron and at 32 was very much an older woman.

Did she have other assets—like money?

Some, one can assume. Like Jann Buss, Christoph may have used his profits in times of prosperity to buy parcels of land and to accumulate other forms of wealth. But whatever he had was unlikely to pass in its entirety to his widow. There would've been nephews, perhaps brothers and uncles lined up to inherit. Still, she took her furniture and perhaps more than a little cash and land as her widow's portion.

Of course, all of these assumptions rest on the evidence of those fine pieces of carved black walnut furniture. The furniture exists still with a bed and a table in the author's house. But did it come into the family with Behrendji? We have only family lore as provenance, and there's this thing about stories that pass from one set of lips to the next. They can be … fanciful.

Another bit of lore about Behrendji is a case in point. We can call it, "The Tale of the Runaway Nobleman's Daughter."

"Once upon a time," my mother began, "long ago in Germany there was the daughter of a baron, a girl named Bertha, who met a handsome young man in the forest. His name was Hermann and he was a miller's son and far below her status. But they fell in love and ran away together to get married. And this is a true story about your great, great, great grandparents. The baron sent his men to bring his daughter back, and no one could protect them. So they had to run far, far away, sailing on a ship across the sea to America where they lived happily ever after."

Later, when I was older, Mom drew her lineage out on paper in the form of a family tree. "The farthest back we can trace our lineage is to Bertha," she said then. "She was the youngest daughter of a nobleman named Baron DeGroot. Her son was my grandfather, Chris."

"And where were they from?" I asked, having never quite bought the story about this child of nobility falling in love with a man who ran a mill. Still, I pictured a Walt Disney-type scene with trysts in woody copses and a mill nestled in trees alongside a millstream, water churning and glistening in the sun as the paddle wheels went round and round.

"Germany, of course."

Of course, where else. I knew Mom's family came from Germany. That wasn't what I'd meant.

"I mean, where in Germany? Like Bavaria or the Rhineland?"

"It might have been Bavaria." Mom didn't know, but Bavaria sounded good to me, too. All those lovely mountains and forests and lakes. Especially, all those fairy tale castles which undoubtedly had housed Bertha's father, which would've made me the great, great-something granddaughter of someone who'd owned a castle. Pretty cool.

Pretty wrong.

But the truth is better, involving real people—hard-working, tough, and resilient people.

The "baron," of course, is Berend, and DeGroot or DeGroth is a common enough surname in Ostfriesland. As for Bertha, Behrendji was eventually to Anglicize her name to Bertha, thereby inadvertently cause my mother a good deal of confusion. Eventually, Behrendji and Bertha were to morph into two separate people, appearing as such on Mom's version of the family tree. And, sadly, the very existence of Ostfriesland in family lore disappeared. For years after this conversation with Mom and throughout my three-year stay in the Rhineland with weekend visits and driving holidays into the north as well as the south of West Germany, I believed that her family probably came from Bavaria.

Oh well. Back to real life.

However they met and whatever the reason—true love, money, or something else—Hermann proposed and Behrendje accepted. They married and, by all accounts, their union would prove a happy one.

With some hurdles along the way. Their domestic thing in 1847 was one such and, by the time Hermann's sister, Theete Lena, left for her new husband's home in her flower-bedecked carriage, Behrendje may have decided she did not want to kill herself trying to run someone else's house for someone else's profit. Why should the fruit of her labor be split among the Müller men? Why should she have to slave night and day to keep house for a bunch of grown men? Why should she direct the servants, cook for the inn, keep the shelves stocked, and do the myriad of jobs that had recently been divided three ways? No. It seems she was clear on this. She wanted her own establishment.

Fortunately, she wasn't the only one who needed resolution. Hermann had been part of his father's household for much too long. He would soon be a middle-aged man and, if he ever intended to run his own affairs, he was going to have to start pretty soon. Although he wouldn't have recognized the expression, Hermann needed to 'get a life.' He might be married to the mill by the church and an accident of birth, he might have to share what he earned from the mill with the church, his father and his brothers, but he could still set up his own associated enterprises.

The answer for both of the Hermann Müllers was to build. So, after his mother's death Hermann bought a piece of village-owned land across the road from the mill. There he built another large, two-story structure. It was a house for Behrendje, plus it would provide new space for a pub and store and barn and give him a degree of independence. He would continue to run the mill and share out its proceeds, but profits from his new enterprises would be his.

It was a tidy solution or would've been if the world had left them alone.

Behrendji and Hermann's house. Photo compliments of Wallrich Müller's great granddaughter, Minna Meinen

Behrendji Berends DeGroot Müller Genealogy

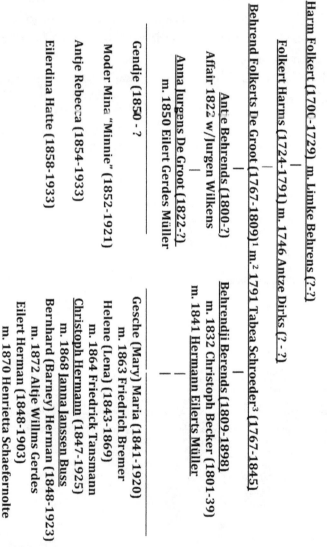

Harm Folkert (1700-1729) m. Limke Behrens (?-?)

Folkert Harms (1724-1791) m. 1746 Antze Dirks (? - ?)

Behrend Folkerts De Groot (1767-1809)[1] m.[2] 1791 Tabea Schroeder[3] (1767-1845)

Antje Behrends (1800-?)
Affair 1822 w/Jurgen Wilkens
Anna Jurgens De Groot (1822-?)
m. 1850 Eilert Gerdes Müller

Gendje (1850 - ?
Moder Mina "Minnie" (1852-1921)
Antje Rebecca (1854-1933)
Eilerdina Hatte (1858-1933)

Behrendji Berends (1809-1898)
m. 1832 Christoph Becker (1801-39)
m. 1841 Hermann Eilerts Müller

Gesche (Mary) Maria (1841-1920)
m. 1863 Friedrich Bremer
Helene (Lena) (1843-1869)
m. 1864 Friedrick Tansmann
Christoph Hermann (1847-1925)
m. 1868 Janna Janssen Buss
Bernhard (Barney) Herman (1848-1923)
m. 1872 Altje Willms Gerdes
Eilert Herman (1848-1903)
m. 1870 Henrietta Schaefernolte

14
Hail Free Friesens

News of momentous historic firsts in far away cities came to the Mill House pub as articles in newspapers—more and more of them as various rulers allowed freedom of the press. Closer to home the people had visible proof that their own rulers in Hannover felt uneasy. Troops moved into Ostfriesland. On many nights the men of Bühren stayed away from the pub. Those were the times the Mill House and its grounds were taken over by soldiers on the march to Aurich or searching for men believed to be preaching sedition or seeking conscripts to build the army's strength.

Mostly, as we've seen, the events that happened elsewhere had no relevance for Ostfriesens and were difficult to understand, revolving as they did around grievances and problems rooted in the past, many of them so obscure that even the people involved had an imperfect grasp of them. Other issues were easy. Serfs in Austria and places like around Wiesbaden in the Duchy of Hesse wanted freedom and a parliament and revolted to get it. A man could wrap his brain around that. On the other hand, the French took to the barricades, seemingly every other day, and who could figure out what made a Frenchman act the way he did.

In Ostfriesland no one had ever entirely taken away the basic human rights, nor had the men—at least those with property—ever lost their right to a say in local affairs. Unless the daily news of uprisings somewhere or other eventually created a ripple effect that reached their doors, the Ostfriesens felt largely uninvolved, more spectator than actor.

But that could change. So men like Hermann read the news from France and Prussia with particular care, watching events elsewhere the way a cornered mouse will eye a hunting snake. They cheered the riots in Berlin and had a good belly laugh reading about disputes between the new rich industrialists and the old landed nobility. They kept a close eye on the way it seemed everyone wanted to set up parliamentary systems … even in Berlin … but particularly that bunch in Frankfurt who had in mind implementing that old post-Napoleonic treaty establishing a German federation governed by a pan-German parliament which would consist of elected officials from every German state.

There were other things. Ideas. A copy of the *New Rhineland News* with its radical editor Karl Marx most likely came their way and would have led to a rousing discussion. Was Marx right? He'd said there'd be spontaneous revolutions of the working man. Well. Didn't that happen just like he said? There'd been uprisings all up and down the Rhine, not to mention in places like Budapest and Saxony and Austria. So what about this idea of redistributing wealth?

The periodic presence of troops in the Uplengen district, though, kept things in proportion while the military, itself, gave them a grievance. Not only were the troops a nuisance and a visible threat within their midst, but the Army of Hannover was in constant need of men, forever on the lookout for boys they could snatch or conscript. It made people angry. Hadn't they always bought their way out of military service to these foreign rulers? Every case of press-ganging threatened to disturb the peace and heightened anger over the poor economy.

An old form of greeting regained popularity and was now heard more often around the pub.

"Eala Frya Fresena," a man would say when joining a group of friends.

"Lever Dod as Slaav," they would respond.

The meaning? "Hail, free Friesens!" and "Better dead than a slave!"

"Eala Frya Fresna!"

Eilert Gerdes Müller, now gray-haired and wizened, had the time and will to sit in council with the other elders of the district discussing what could be done. He most likely took part in writing petitions and participated in delegations complaining about troops, demanding road repairs, doing the work of representing the community in Aurich. They had some successes, too. For a time their pressure led to troops being withdrawn from Uplengen, but an uptick in revolutionary action elsewhere brought them back again.

Hermann, too, no doubt took a hand, going with his father to Aurich to complain to the district authorities over damages done by the troops he'd been forced to billet and the constant threat of conscription that hung over his younger brothers. The two men likely came home with more promises than action. That would have to do. But they probably did secure certificates exempting the Müller men from military service. None of this, though, would have made up for the inconvenience and the nervous strain of housing groups of violent and often drunk men, for the trees lost when soldiers cut them down for firewood, for productive animals slaughtered indiscriminately to make meals for troops.

Eilert Gerdes and Hermann would both have participated in debates over the status of their country. Should Ostfriesland take advantage of the turmoil to declare her own independence? No one questioned their status as a separate people who'd owned their own land since the beginning of time or the facts that they had their own culture, their own traditional system of government, and their own language—albeit they no longer spoke Friisian but had adopted Plattdeutsch, a language they shared in common with most of the low-lying areas of the Baltic and North Sea regions. Elsewhere in Europe men were hassling over the same issues. The men elected to the pan-German parliament in Frankfurt preached the gospel of a democratic confederation of Germanic states. They said they were there "at the will of the people" to write a constitution for this federation and would eventually govern it. BUT ... One thing no two people could agree on—what states would make up the confederation? What did it mean to be a German?

The Ostfriesens saw themselves as being potentially victimized by that point. They were no more German than were the Saxons of England or the West Friesens of The Netherlands or the North Friesens of Denmark. They thought of themselves as a large non-German minority within Hannover. But Hermann and Eilert Gerdes were quite certain that their opinion was of no interest to the men in Frankfurt.

Geopolitics was probably a word they'd never used, but they knew the principle of the thing, knew that up in Frankfurt as well as in Berlin and Hannover, itself, the men painting colors on Europe's map would splash whatever hue they used for Germany over Ostfriesland's territory. Of course they would. How not? Ostfriesland was nothing but a sliver of coastal land and islands between the rest of so-called Germany and the North Sea. No matter how big or how small this state of Germany became, geopolitics and Ostfriesland's lack of any sort of power meant its territory would be subsumed within that of the new Germany.

News of more revolutions reached Bühren, stories of more fighting in the streets of cities as far away as Budapest and Warsaw with more stories of places like Hungary trying to break away from Vienna and seeming for a time to succeed. If the Hungarians could do it, if Berliners could revolt, could the Ostfriesens? To what end? Then with that question hanging in the air, the armies were ordered out of their barracks and turned loose on the dissidents. The ruling class that had seemed cowed one minute reacted the next by arresting and executing revolutionaries, a cycle that extended right across Europe and that would be followed by more riots and revolts, by more arrests and executions. Concessions would be made; concessions would be withdrawn.

The men of Bühren and Remels talked of this on nights when the Mill House was free of troops. They sat in their usual places, smoked their pipes and drank their beer or sometimes something stronger, raised their voices and shouted, "You mark my words! No good will come of this." Then came something they'd all known was in the offing—news of revolts in the provinces of Schleswig and Holstein just to their north and east on the Danish peninsula and home to the North Friesens. The issues there were complex and deep-rooted, so much so that even many of the Germans, Danes, and North Friesens who lived in those two provinces had only the loosest of grasps on them.

Simplified, the Danish government considered the semi-independent duchies of Schleswig and Holstein nominally subject to whoever ruled Denmark and that was an end of it. The Germans in those two provinces, on the other hand, believed they had a legal and moral right to a complete break with Copenhagen and to join the German confederation if they chose. The ethnic Germans took to the streets to make their point. The Frankfurt Parliament declared in their favor. The Danes reacted by blockading all of the nearby ports belonging to German states, including Ostfriesland's Em River estuary. The Frankfurt Parliament responded by asking Prussia to rush to the aid of their fellow Germans.

The Prussians—always interested in annexing Schleswig and Holstein—did just that, marching north from Hannover, the army passing within a few days ride of Uplengen.

"You watch," the men said. "They won't get away with it. This'll bring the British back. They'll never let Berlin steal Schleswig-Holstein."

Indeed the British did intervene. Along with France and Russia they forced the parties to negotiations in Malmo, presenting them with an agreement. There would be a ceasefire, a demilitarization, and a shared administration of the two provinces.

"They'll never agree to that in Frankfurt and Berlin." The men could all rally around that statement, too, and they were both right and wrong. Prussia ignored the Malmo accord. For its part, the Frankfurt parliament voted ratification, eventually, but the people of Frankfurt didn't. They rioted and murdered two parliamentarians. This event sparked off a yet another round of violence that spread through the Germanic states.

It made for great discussions. It filled news columns. The Danish blockade, the Prussian army passing through Hannover, and the North Friesens caught again in a geopolitical vise—it was all very exciting but only marginally relevant in Uplengen. Still any fool could see that all those princes and kings and dukes and such … were just waiting until the idiots in Frankfurt got tired or killed each other off, or starved to death or whatever.

"You watch," the old men said. "His Majesty will serve up that parliament as sauce on his Christmas goose. It'll be business as usual or worse in Berlin." They were talking about Prussia's King Frederick William IV, who would pretty much do just that.

We Go to America, 1854

The economy was improving the year Hermann and Behrendje moved their family, which had just grown by the addition of a son, into their new house. Travelers appeared more frequently. The price of tobacco went down. They could get tea, again. With their beverage of choice—that good black brew—on the table, how could the year not be a good one?

Christoph had been born with little fuss, and Behrendje was soon pregnant again. A year later after a much more difficult delivery, she produced a pair of twins they named Eilert and Bernard. Neither mother nor twins, however, came through unscathed. Bernard would carry a crippling birth-related injury for life. His mother would have no more children.

Back in the old family home, the youngest of Hermann's brothers, Gerhard Eylerts, apparently saw no future in Ostfriesland and decamped for America becoming part of the great exodus. He was young ... just nineteen ... and had probably hoped to see more change for the better coming out of the revolutionary fervor of the past few years. It's also likely that with the devolution of power to Berlin he saw the handwriting on the wall. Prussia's army was growing, and for a young man of his age, conscription was inevitable. Like many others, he voted with his feet and left the country.

Or there might have been one more motivation for his departure in March of 1849. It seems Behrendji had brought a pretty young woman into the old mill house—one Anna Jurgen Wilkins. Whether Anna first arrived as a servant or a dependent (and when) is as wrapped in mystery as her childhood.

This is where we get back to Antje Berends DeGroot, Anna Jurgen's mother. While it's possible that Antje was the daughter of another Berend DeGroot, the strong circumstantial evidence of dates and places and names points to Antje being one of Behrendji's older siblings, making Behrendji Anna's aunt.

What do I know about Antje? Not much except that she had an affair with Jurgen Wilkens, who didn't marry her. He did, however, end up with his name on a birth certificate as the resulting child's father. And, so, Anna was born and, eventually, arrived at the mill house.

She was a lively presence, an attractive girl with all of the right assets in the right places. Plus, she had spunk and exuded good will. People liked her, enjoyed her chatter, her bright intelligence, and her laughter.

In the case of Eilert Gerdes, her impact on the family was obvious.

Eilert Gerdes had lost his wife but it's unlikely he'd been sleeping alone. Like many relatively rich men of his time, he enjoyed more from the female servants than just the performance of daily household chores. And so it was. For some time—at least beginning six months after Gerhard Eylerts left for America and probably earlier—he'd been sexually active with young Anna. That he'd "taken advantage" of a young woman in his household was no surprise. Such was common. That he'd marry a servant and an illegitimate woman even though she was pregnant? No.

A pregnant servant might be turned out into the streets. She might be sent home and allowed back once her child was born and left behind. A man might admit to being the father (if he was sure he was) and allow his name to be used on the birth certificate as Anna's genetic father had. But marriage? Not likely. Not unless, for example, she was Behrendji's niece.

Even so, his sons could not have been happy about their father's choice of bedmates, and the affair might even have sent young Eylerts Gerhard sailing off to America. Otherwise, the fact that the old man was enjoying a young woman's body was no big deal. But Anna and marriage? And more children? Legitimate children who could have a claim on the estate? Because by Christmas of 1849, Anna was very obviously pregnant and she was young, and she could be expected to have many children.

Which suited Eilert Gerdes just fine. With a smile if not a smirk on his face, Eilert Gerdes married Anna in March of 1850. Four months later, on a warm July day, she delivered a healthy child and with it a new family began in the old mill house. Happily, Eilert Gerdes set about siring his third batch of children, this lot as clogged with girls as his last had been with boys. Before all was said and done and he died in 1858, he and Anna would have four daughters.

Besides getting married, Eilert Gerdes had discovered that he enjoyed being a family and village elder a lot more than he did riding herd on his farms and businesses. Dealing with his boys, all of whom seemed to think they knew more than him, was just plain tiring. He decided to retire and devote his time to public service. While he still lived off the proceeds of his properties, he left their management to Hermann (the mill) and Wallrich (the inn and restaurant). The two sons paid their father a percentage of their profits, of course, and the old man and his growing family continued to live in the Mill House where Anna was the mistress and Wallrich ran the Mill House businesses. Wallrich probably took over more of the farming, as well.

Behrendje continued to manage her own house, raised her children, and probably felt great satisfaction. She'd brought her own furniture out of storage when she'd moved into her new home, and she now had a well-furnished establishment she could call her own and show off with pride. There were carpets for the floors and the beautifully carved walnut furnishings. She could afford curtains for the windows plus her new house had all the modern conveniences. These probably included the latest in porcelain stoves, an indoor water pump in the kitchen and a separate closet for bathing. There would be no more hauling water by the bucket load for her, and there was the luxury of a hot bath in complete privacy. Best of all, there was music. She most likely installed a piano in her parlor, and it's probable that Hermann's violin—an early Stradivarius—was often heard in the evenings.

Gesche Maria and Lena, her daughters, were growing and took up a good deal of Behrendje's time. They, after all, needed educating in a woman's skills as well as help learning to read, write, and do their numbers. A new and prosperous Ostfriesen middle class had come into being in the past few decades, one composed not just of people who'd made money but who had educations. She'd heard the men joke about women getting too much learning for their own good and laugh about women who could do more than sign their name and count their egg money, but to Behrendje it was not funny.

Her girls would be raised to be the equal of anyone they might meet. They would be welcome in any house. Already, they showed signs of having the natural asset of beauty. If Behrendje had anything to do about it, they would also become accomplished. They would read, do their numbers, understand the world around them, play the piano, and sing.

Then there were her boys. Thank God they were healthy and sturdy, although Bernard was having difficulty learning to walk. Still, he was a clever little fellow.

Altogether Behrendje would have been happy.

Over in the old house, Anna, regularly pregnant, reigned supreme. She, too, had every reason to be satisfied with her situation. She was mistress of her own domain and what a splendid domain it was. Of course, her day's work was never done what with the steady flow of business coming into the inn, the care of her girls, and the management of the maids that Wallrich hired to help out. "It's easier just to do it myself," she may well have said with a laugh while sending a girl back to do some chore over again. The main thing was: Anna's little girls were healthy and her husband prosperous.

Then in 1853 Wallrich married. Rather than installing his new wife in the old house with Anna and her first two daughters, he moved with his bride, Grietje, to an ancestral property she brought to the marriage. This left Hermann as the sole master of the mill and its related businesses.

Out in the world, the chaos of the past few years had given way to a new normal but in the process the dislocations combined with glowing reports from America meant a huge uptick in emigration. Every village, hamlet, and town in Ostfriesland had lost families to America while handling émigrés had become big business in the port cities. New laws dealing with emigration had been passed in Hannover, while the American authorities had begun thinking they needed to do something to control the flow.

The flood of letters and news articles from America just grew. And all of those people were writing home to encourage their friends, neighbors, and family members to join them. Plus the

American railroad companies had been granted huge tracts of land in exchange for building their rail lines and were advertising that land for sale in German-language newspapers. And if that wasn't enough, there was free land to be had as well.

No evening went by without a letter or news article coming into Hermann's pub in someone's pocket to be read to everyone.

Year after year Hermann had been hearing about life in America. He knew there probably were as many lies and exaggerations as truth. A man could have as much land as he could work? He could make a fortune in the gold fields or own a ranch in Texas or get rich with the railroads? Reports of the new land didn't just glow, they glittered as bright and tempting to the eyes of otherwise sober men as a piece of gilded paper to a crow. Hermann doubted it all.

Still, there had to be truth below all the razzle-dazzle. This is what he seemed to believe: in America hard work was rewarded. In America a man had scope to use his initiative to create and exploit opportunity.

Hermann made up his mind.

In 1854, he sold his holdings, turned over his tenancy rights on the mill to his brother Wallrich, who also bought Hermann's adjacent land, house, pub and store. Then, working through an agent, Hermann made all the necessary arrangements. Unlike the Buss and Franken families of six years earlier, he would not travel in steerage and he would know his destination. The ship was the *O Thyen*, a large, three-masted sailing ship. The place was Quincy, Illinois. On 4 September 1854, the Hermann Müllers—Hermann listing himself as a "merchant"—set sail from the port of Bremen, traveling in the relative comfort of their own second class cabin. With them went Behrendje's furniture, Hermann's violin, and trunks of other belongings.

The *O Thyen* was a considerable step up from The *Elizabeth*, the ship that carried the Buss and Franken families across six years earlier. It was substantially larger and carried a great deal more sail. Besides the steerage deck which held 238 passengers in conditions similar to those of all passengers on the *Elizabeth*, it had a second-class deck of individual cabins for another 84 passengers. The remaining 17 passengers enjoyed first class cabins, notable for their larger size. All passengers were given their meals on the *O Thyen*.

The first twenty days of their crossing was rough, the *O Thyen* under her master, Charles H. Addicks, fought one storm after another, struggling just to stay alive in the early winter seas. The 329 passengers aboard—especially the 238 in steerage—must have been more than miserable. During that period the meals provided by the ship's cooks were mostly cold as was everyone aboard. One sailor went overboard and one child died during these bad days. The weather smoothed out toward the end of September, the captain ordered a full complement of sail set, and the ship got on its proper course, its passengers eventually catching glimpses of Cuba. Still, four more passengers died before, on 8 November 1854, the *O Thyen* reached New Orleans, cleared customs, and the Müllers continued up the Mississippi.

15
Christoph

Hermann Müller's oldest son, Christoph, was seven when their side-wheeled steamer pulled to a stop below Quincy's limestone bluffs. As the roustabouts set the gangway, Chris would have peered over the railing at the mud flats, at the web of trees fringing what was visible of an island, and at the wide expanse of river. What would he have seen? There were holes in the cliff faces—dark, gaping, entrances to what? Caves, of course? With hidden treasures? And along the river there'd be frogs and fish, birds and bird eggs. Looking down, he would've seen the usual compliment of boys gathered on the bank watching the boat swing to a stop. Some of them were barefoot, their toes curling in the muck. Chris must've known it right then. He'd found heaven.

His was a "Boy's World" youth. His growing up during years alongside the Mississippi might have served as a model for the fictional life of Tom Sawyer, a story set just across the river from Quincy and a few decades later. Chris would have had chores to do but would also have had time to run wild through the dirt streets of the small port, to play games with friends, explore the limestone caves, fish along the creeks and river, and hunt the surrounding country. School was part of his life during the winter months but, while his mother preached the value of education, and he would send seven of his own ten children through college, book learning did not loom large in his list of early priorities.

Then, when Chris was twelve, the idyll in Quincy ended. The year before his grandfather Müller had died back in Bühren and his step-grandmother Anna with four daughters had emigrated, staying with them for a time. It was strange, but those little girls were all his aunts. "Half-aunts," his mother had told him.

"So, which half's my aunt?" he might well have asked, as fresh boys do. "Her right side or her left?"

And the adults would laugh and say, "Cheeky little brute."

He wouldn't have had much interest in Anna's stories about the things going on back in Bühren. He'd only been seven when they left. So, Anna talked to his parents about his grandfather's last days and his death, about his Uncle Wallrich who was now, as the miller, the head of the Müller family, about his new cousins and about who'd built what and who was living where and things like that. Anna was a vibrant woman with lots of news to convey.

Why had she decided to emigrate with her children? It wasn't the sort of thing women did on their own, particularly not mothers with young ones. Doubtless she had reasons she could share and, Anna being Anna, she might even have told them flat out that there was a shortage of enterprising bachelors at home but not in America. How long would she have had to sleep alone in the Old Mill House before she found a man to marry? And what kind of a man might that be?

It was a problem these days back in Ostfriesland, a country decimated of men by emigration. Anna had faced it squarely, made her choice, and took herself and her girls to America where they could all marry prosperous, propertied men. Which they all did. In the meantime, Anna needed a job.

She'd not been in Quincy long when her search for employment brought her news of a recently widowed man in the

Ostfriesen community at South Prairie. "They say he is a good man who needs a woman to care for his children and his house, and I have found a wagon that will take me and my girls there," she told her in-laws, or words to that effect.

And just like that, as suddenly as she'd arrived, she was gone.

Almost as fast, or so it seemed in retrospect, she announced she'd be remarrying—not to her employer but to a young man of good Ostfriesen stock that she'd met in South Prairie. In 1859, the South Prairie town that would become Golden was still more hamlet than village, was just a collection of buildings that had moved from its earlier location to take up space alongside the North Star Railroad tracks at a point where the Chicago, Burlington, and Quincy Railway had bought right-of-ways. The CB&Q tracks from Chicago, if built, would cross the North Star tracks going to Quincy at Golden.

Hermann and Behrendji Müller with children

Hermann and Behrendje, of course, traveled to Golden to attend the wedding which was held in the newly built village church. There, the Müllers met everyone, were made to feel welcome, and were soon persuaded to make the new town their home. Here, Hermann was told, was a golden opportunity. Goods could be shipped in cheaply and efficiently by rail and there was a market of over 300 families needing supplies of every nature.

It was just nine short years since Jann and Ickka's initial land purchase, and already the community that had followed them had spawned a commercial and social core. It also had acquired its own name—Keokuk Junction—and a smock mill, one completed just three years earlier by an Ostfriesen named Heinrich A. Emminga. The presence of the mill, that wonderful touch of home, and the finding of kindred spirits in the Emmingas probably sealed the deal for Hermann. In 1859, Hermann took a chance that the South Prairie hamlet would become a junction town and built a store in the young settlement.

While the Müllers were Ostfriesen, like almost everyone else now in and around the Plattdeutsch-speaking Keokuk Junction, they would likely have been seen as "not quite one of us" by the majority of Ostfriesens who were farmers. But this was no different than at home where they'd been lumped into the merchant class. Still, there was a Lutheran church, a religion they all shared in common, and there were a few other merchants with families to provide a small social life, and there was their own language. Hermann would not be the first to engage in general commerce in the new village, but he aimed to be the best.

The Müllers represented another change in the South Prairie community. In the first years the families who came to South Prairie were almost all related in one way or another. But word had spread at home as well as through the German communities up and down the Mississippi. Quincy was already known as

New Ostfriesland, a mecca for Plattdeutsch-speaking, Lutheran families. Soon, other Ostfriesens, who'd begun their American experience in Quincy, saw new opportunities in South Prairie and elsewhere in Illinois and began settling villages like Keokuk Junction and the surrounding prairie.

This is not to forget the "English" (as the Ostfriesens still called their neighbors) living in the area who'd done so much to welcome and help their new Ostfriesen neighbors. They, too, were part of the mix, and soon Keokuk Junction had a Reformed Presbyterian church and congregations of other denominations, and the town became partly bi-lingual.

Hermann no doubt sought Ickka and Jann's friendship and patronage before he built his store. The Busses were a founding family, a force in the Emanuel South Prairie Lutheran Church, and their good will would have been important to Hermann if he and Behrendje (who had Anglicized her name and was now being called Bertha) expected to prosper in the community. Hermann and Jann, having much in common, might even have become friends if circumstances had allowed it. Bertha and Ickka (who they all called Moder)? Not so much.

To start with Bertha had adapted her name to the tongues of her English friends in Quincy. Ickka wouldn't have dreamed of such a thing. Then, Bertha was ten years older, essentially of another generation. Additionally, Bertha was comfortable with town life and had left what acquaintance she'd had, if any, with farming and animal husbandry far behind. In short the two women shared a language and a culture but little else.

It's not that Bertha would've looked down on Ickka, in fact she probably admired her inordinately and would have spoken of her in glowing terms. It's more that Ickka with her work-roughened hands and oft-mended clothes never felt the need to take on the trappings or graces of the wealth she and Jann were accumulating. She and Bertha shared their core values but little else. For both women their past and the strong economic class system they'd grown up in separated them and made a friendship difficult. That, however, probably changed in their later years as circumstances brought them together and as they shared an entire tribe of grandchildren. Perhaps after Bertha was widowed and went to live with her oldest son and his wife, Ickka's daughter, they even became good friends.

In the meantime back in Keokuk Junction in 1859 and the years immediately after, the CB&Q had laid its tracks where expected, a saloon joined the blacksmith shop and church, the government built a post office, a hotel sprang up, Hermann Müller had his general store, and the town added three more Lutheran churches. One of these was called the Emmanuel (Keokuk Junction) Lutheran Church and comprised those individuals from Ickka's congregation who lived in and around town and who'd had a difficult time commuting.

The move meant the end of childhood for Chris. He worked in the store. He worked on a farm Hermann also bought. He went to the South Prairie Lutheran Church on Sunday where he kept an eye on the girls. He served Ickka's pretty daughter, Janna, in the store and slipped her pieces of candy when no one was looking. But to him, five years her senior, she was just a kid.

There were other girls around, though, and it was with them that he exchanged flirtatious glances, it was with them he danced on May Day. He grew tall, towering in photos over his family, his blue eyes direct, his face handsome by anyone's standards.

In the midst of this growing up time, when Chris was sixteen, General P.G.T. Beauregard of the Confederate forces fired on a Union garrison at Fort Sumter. The United States was at war with itself. President Abraham Lincoln, an Illinois lawyer, called upon the people of his home state to supply armed militia regiments to augment the professional Union army. Recruiters appeared in Golden—Keokuk Junction having been renamed yet again but finally finding a name it would keep—and other Ostfriesen communities and, for the most part, left empty handed.

The same was not true of the state at large or of the larger Germanic émigré population. In the next few years, Illinois fielded 150 infantry, 17 horse, and 2 light artillery regiments holding some 250,000 men. Three of the infantry regiments were composed of German speakers.

Where were the Ostfriesens in all of this?

Before addressing that question, there is an issue of definition. For thousands of years as we've discussed, Ostfriesens saw themselves as a distinct people and, definitely, not a Germanic tribe. Gradually, though, the line blurred. Ostfriesens had given up their language in favor of the lingua franca of their region—Plattdeutsch. Next, as a minority living on a fringe of land, they'd been subsumed by more powerful, mostly Germanic, neighbors. Then, those who'd come to America had seen themselves lumped together with other Plattdeutch speakers as "Germans." Finally and more subtly, there was a general assumption among English speakers that the translation of Plattdeutsch as "Low German" meant a language of the lower classes rather than referring to inhabitants of low-lying land.

So, what with one thing and another, it was just easier for Ostfriesens in America to go with the flow, claim Hochdeutsch, which after all was the language of liturgy, as their own, and refer to themselves as German until the inevitable happened. Their offspring forgot their actual origins.

Under the heading of "you are what you're called," that's exactly how things were evolving, and Union recruiters could be forgiven for seeing the people of South Prairie as ethnic Germans. Yet, the conversion was not yet complete so recruiters, expecting to be welcomed there as they had been in Germanic communities, were in for a shock. While people like Hermann might let themselves be called Germans, they weren't. He like other first generation Ostfriesen men on the prairies of Illinois had escaped being conscripted into the Prussian army. Their fathers and grandfathers had done the same with other armies. Ostfriesens did not willingly serve in the armies of foreign military powers. So, why should they go off to fight in the Union Army or the CSA, for that matter? Where was their bone in this struggle?

Which brings up another issue. Did the men of South Prairie feel any involvement, any allegiance to their new country or to the issues?

As the conflict exploded in Kansas, it became obvious in nearby central Illinois that the fiery rhetoric between slave-based and industrial-based economies was creating its own momentum. Just as they had in the bad years of the late 1840's, the Ostfriesens read their newspapers, watched and listened, hearing the 'Englishers' around them talking.

Mostly these neighbors were just like the Ostfriesens with farms no bigger than one family could manage, unlike those damn southern slave-owners who'd spilled into Illinois and were buying up huge swatches of land. Everyone could see that the newcomers with their slaves could afford to undercut the man who worked for himself. This threat to their income and way of life gave farming people an economic incentive to call for abolition in Illinois. Otherwise, as concerned the institution of slavery, it wasn't that anyone particularly wanted abolition or believed in the rights of all men to be free. For South Prairie as for other areas of agrarian Illinois, people just didn't want slave-based agriculture out-producing and out-selling them.

That said, the Ostfriesens of South Prairie and, particularly, the young men like Chris and like Gerhard Buss, decided this conflict had nothing to do with them. They were wrong.

PART THREE
BUSS & MILLER CLAN

Janna Buss and Chris Miller

16
Ickka on Her Own

The appraiser appointed by the State of Illinois came shortly after Jann Buss died. Snow lay deep on the ground, but the sun shone coldly over the prairie. If you didn't look too closely at smoke rising from chimneys or know about the vanished forested patches, you might imagine melting snow would reveal a land unchanged for eons. But change had come to South Prairie on a massive scale. The old land was gone, razed by man's hand, stripped, drained, planted, and transformed. The new inhabitants considered this all to the good; called it "progress." They hadn't raped the vanished prairie, they'd tamed it … set it to doing good.

The day of the appraisal in mid-February 1859 found the Buss family still living in the rude one-room log cabin they'd purchased a decade earlier, albeit a cabin improved by excellent calking, a wood floor and glass in the small front windows. Unlike other immigrant pioneers Jann had seen no reason to build his wife a frame house. Or, perhaps, it'd been Ickka's decision to plough their profits back into the farm. After all, they had what they needed, an opinion Ickka obviously held—witness that she opted to stay in the cabin for yet another decade.

More seriously, Jann had failed to make provisions for his family should he die prematurely … had done nothing about writing a will.

He'd known the need. He'd lived in Illinois for a decade, and he'd no doubt bought tools and livestock cheap because of other people's tragedies, attending the estate auctions that accompanied every intestate death. He had to have known that Illinois inheritance laws mandated the sale of earthly goods in such cases along with the apportionment of the profits by percentages to the heirs. He had to have known the consequences. But he'd seen no reason to protect his family from those laws. Or, possibly, like many, he just kept postponing the task as though by blocking it from his conscious mind and keeping it off his daily schedule he was actually performing a type of sympathetic magic.

So long as we do nothing, nothing will happen. Don't look, and the grim reaper will pass on by.

But death very obviously and remorselessly makes its own magic and comes at its own time. And whatever the reason, one winter day the government appraiser appeared at Ickka's door with his portable writing table, his pen and ink, and his supply of paper, most of which would not be needed. His list would be very short. He started in the low loft, climbing a ladder to get there and stooping to look around and probably cursing because the climb had been a waste of time. There would have been nothing for his paper up there. He most likely saw straw pallets laid out for the boys and covered with fading quilts. A few pegs set into the walls would have held the boys' well-worn and patched Sunday clothes.

Downstairs the girls most likely shared a bed in one corner; Jann and Ickka would have used another—both beds doubling as seating when company came as they had since that first Sunday "service." The appraiser counted the beds, all two of them. Cooking was done on a wood stove placed strategically near the fireplace in a kitchen corner. He made a note. One stove. Water came from an outside hand pump, brought into the house by the bucket load. He could see that bathing would be done on a Saturday night, would be nothing more than a sponge bath actually, one taken standing in a copper tub set in front of the fireplace—water hot for the first user and cold for the last. An outhouse—known even then as the "little house behind the house"—would serve the other sanitation necessity with a slop jar stored under a bed in case of emergency or for use in a particularly bad blizzard.

He did not count the bucket, the tub, or the slop jar.

Ickka's household inventory as eventually enumerated by the appraiser was: a stove, a clock, a table, one cupboard, a clothes press, two beds and one crib. Ickka also had bedding and mattresses. The rest of her things were lumped together as necessary household and kitchen items. She was allowed to keep these along with a spinning wheel, a loom, a pair of cards, and unitemized wearing apparel for herself and her children valued at $85.

There were none of the possessions most American women in this period considered important. There were no comfortable chairs with backs for sitting of an evening or even a deep tub for bathing. There were no carpets for the floors. Ickka did not have a sink or a counter for food preparation. And, most of all, there was no privacy beyond old quilts used to divide off the beds at night.

For all its meagerness the cabin was cozy, required little maintenance, and offered a certain efficiency. It was only a few steps between fireplace and stove, between table and cupboard or between these and the door. The trestle table with its benches (considered kitchen furniture and not itemized) would have been the heart of the family. There the family ate, the children did their homework, food was chopped and mixed, Ickka figured up her accounts and laid out cloth for new clothes or mended or darned. The spinning wheel most likely stood near the fire, while a butter churn (one of those household necessities) sat next to the door. Pegs driven into the walls held coats while the clothes press contained what spare shirts, skirts, and pants the family possessed. Shelves above the stove supported pots, pans, and crocks and were ladened as well with preserves. Herbs most likely hung conveniently from the ceiling beams while twists of onions, bags of potatoes and carrots, hams, and other foodstuffs preserved on the farm were stored in the smoke house or down in an adjacent root cellar. We assume Ickka had both.

Alongside the smoke house, Ickka would have had a barn of some sort, a pig sty, and a chicken house plus fenced pens and appurtenances for her livestock. Of these the State of Illinois let her keep: one milch cow and calf, one horse, one woman's saddle and bridle, food provisions for her family worth $100, sheep worth $27, fleeces worth $5, a three-month supply of food for her animals, and a three-month supply of fuel. In total her inheritance was valued at $465.

She bought the following back at the estate auction: 1 lot old irons and stanchions, 1 culling machine, 1 culling box, 1 horse, 1 yoke oxen, 2 cows, 1 knife, 1 old saw, 1 poor cow, 1 yearling heifer, and 18 hogs, paying a grand total of $226. During the auction she lost a number of small farm implements plus two plows, a carriage, a mule, a mare, and a tea kettle. These went to other buyers.

What hasn't been enumerated was Jann's most important possession, the reason for all the sacrifice and struggle—his land. It should have gone to auction, too. It didn't. At some undocumented point in the process, Ickka reached an agreement with the state about the land. There's no record of how she accomplished the feat, and speculation just leads to more questions. The fact remains, in a period when women needed men to cosign on purchases of real goods like land, Ickka Eilert Buss somehow obtained sole ownership of her farmland.

Jann had died in early February. The estate was settled expeditiously, the auction and other details concluded by early March. The small prairie flowers that bloom close to the ground and proliferate in their shy fashions were just making their appearances as the state officials went away, and Ickka was left to get on with things. She had her land, animals, children, meager possessions, and three-month supply of feed and fuel designed to tide her over until the weather moderated or until she remarried.

Which was the question. Would she remarry? What would happen next?

Ickka was thirty-seven years old and a matron, her body worn down with child bearing and hard work, with exposure to the sun and wind. Her hands, already beginning to show arthritic changes, looked like they belonged to a sixty-year-old, but her hair under its ubiquitous cap or bonnet remained alive with color, and her eyes had lost none of their determined spark. She was as slow to speak as ever but when she did, when she raised her eyes to look squarely into another's, that person listened. If that person happened to be one of her children, they not only listened but moved with alacrity to obey.

She wasn't an easy person to know despite her good works in the church and her quiet conformity to most community values and mores. She wasn't a beautiful woman nor was she young. Still, she was known as a hard worker and there were men— some of them younger—who would have been glad to marry her for her land and her community stature. In fact, custom dictated that she must remarry to give her children a father and her farm a man to run it.

No doubt, as was the way with these things in a rural area just emerging from its pioneering period, men who'd lost their wives and had children that needed a mother would've found excuses to visit her farm, would've performed small services, and would've sat down to dinner at her table under the glowering eyes of her oldest son.

Actually, meals during those first weeks would have been served with more than a little tension while the hole that Jann's death left was closing and while various expectations and ambitions played themselves out. On a normal day, if any of those days was normal, Ickka would've presided over a table set for seventeen-year-old Gerd, sixteen-year-old Elsche Catharina, twelve-year-old Heinrich, nine-year-old Johann, seven-year-old Janna, six-year-old Gesche, four-year-old Weert, and two-year-old Eilert. The youngest perhaps were confused and grieving. But the rest? We don't know, but they had to have been plagued by the questions: What would happen next? What would become of them?

The oldest boy, Gerhard 'Gerd' Jannsen Buss, probably hoped … perhaps expected, maybe even demanded … that he move to the head of the table and take his father's seat and exercise his authority and his rights. Under Salic law (followed in a loose way in Ostfriesland in that period) he was the heir, not his mother. Even under American law, he ought to share the estate. Besides, he was certainly old enough and experienced enough to take over his father's farm duties and responsibilities.

More, for Gerhard, the farm was essentially all he knew. He'd trekked into Clayton Township and been with his father during every stage of the selection of and negotiation for the farm. He'd seen the plows break up the prairie. He'd slaved for the farm and been a major factor in creating its current prosperity.

Except for time off for essential schooling and church, his days had been totally ordered by farm work. Plus, it was Gerhard who went with his father to get their grain ground at the mill in Quincy, who had learned to get good prices for their products, who sat in the town's taverns with him and debated new farming techniques. Plus, he, not his mother, kept up with the critical events of the times that could affect how the farm was run.

In fact, as we're seen, there were such events afoot. The trouble brewing between north and south was coming to a head. Only four months before Jann died, he'd most likely taken Gerhard and Heinrich into Quincy to listen in Washington Park to Abraham Lincoln debate a man who'd been their county circuit court judge—Stephen Douglas. Gerhard probably had heard Lincoln, the Springfield lawyer, say:

"I have no purpose to introduce political and social equality between the white and black races. There is a physical difference between the two, which, in my judgment, will probably forever forbid their living together on the footing of perfect equality, and inasmuch as it becomes a necessity that there must be a difference, I, as well as Judge Douglas, am in favor of the race to which I belong having the superior position."

Like others, Gerhard probably hadn't followed a lot of the argument between the two men but that didn't matter. He had no intention of fighting over the North-South issues. No. The bottom line for him was completely personal. When and if war came, his family would need a strong hand at the helm to guide it through whatever might befall. His hand.

Had he made a few other assumptions both before and after his father's death? Of course he had. How not? It was his right to replace Jann everywhere but in his mother's bed.

The last bit was the problem—the marital bed. As the

state intestate process rolled on and it became obvious that his mother—not him—would acquire ownership of the land, the matter of his mother's marital status became critical. If she remained single and if she followed custom, the farm would not be divided among the siblings but would come intact to him either in the near future by deed or when his mother died. His responsibility, then, would be to see to it that his siblings had a good start in life.

But if his mother remarried, then under Illinois law when she died the new husband would acquire her property and all bets would be off. Worse. What if she had more children by this man? The idea of his mother having sex was undoubtedly abhorrent, but he had to think of these things. It'd only been two years since Eilert was born, and there was no doubt—his mother was a very fertile woman. These were not thoughts he wanted to have but, lying on his rude straw pallet at night with his brothers sleeping around him, Gerhard perhaps ground his teeth, certainly considered the unimaginable, and made his plans.

It's unlikely that Ickka left her son in suspense for long. She'd certainly decided—perhaps as far back as the day it looked like Jann might die of the bee stings—that with the loss of one husband and master she wouldn't willingly take another. Thus, as the appraiser made his lists, as the February winds howled their relentless way across the prairie and whined through the eaves, gusting down the chimney and threatening to tear the roof off the outhouse, she may have assured Gerhard on that one point. There'd be no new man in the house. She may also made another of her decisions quite clear—no man would run the farm or govern the family. Not Gerhard. Not another husband.

"I will farm," Ickka told her children in one form or another.

"You will help. This way we will all eat."

The subject was not up for discussion and was probably presented without consideration for the feelings or sensitivities, whatever these might've been, of her offspring. There would've been no negotiating, no accommodating, no sense that Gerhard or his siblings had a voice in her decisions or in the extra chores that would now fall on their shoulders.

This was the way of the time. Families were organized along authoritarian lines. Children had a choice of obeying their parents or of leaving and making their own way in the world which, of course, many did. There was war coming and uniforms to be worn. There was gold to be dug in California and cowboying in the Wild West. There was cheap land and free land and great adventures to be lived. Girls and boys alike, dissatisfied with farm life or poverty or parents, set off with their small packs to make their fortunes.

Thirteen- and fourteen-year-old boys joined the U.S. Army as drummers and buglers. They got jobs as drivers and clerks, as cleaners and stable boys. Girls dressed as boys and drove stagecoaches, took out homesteads, some would fight in the Confederate and Union armies. More were reduced to working as dance hall girls and prostitutes.

Both Gerhard and the next oldest, Heinrich, could easily have rolled up a blanket, grabbed some provisions, and set out for a new life and a stab at making a fortune. To Ickka's credit, they didn't. All of her children stayed with her until they left to start their own families. And it would be twenty-eight years before the first of them would even leave South Prairie.

They stayed because Ickka needed them. They stayed because their ties were to the Plattdeutsch-speaking, Lutheran community. Perhaps they stayed in part immediately after Jann's death because war was coming. Then, too, the boys may have been influenced by the other thing Ickka had decided.

She must have said to them something like, "There is to be no confusion. This is my land, and I will decide what to do with it. But when you are grown, I will help each of you buy a farm to get started in your own life and that will be the end of my responsibilities to you. As for you girls, when you marry you will go to live with your husband."

Why am I certain she planned in this way?

Ickka would never know it, but she'd started something. Substitute the word "college" for "farm" and give equal opportunity to the girls and the concept would be repeated by Ickka's daughter Janna to her children and by the youngest of those children, Willie, to his and by Ickka's great grandchild, Marolyn, to us. Ickka would've nodded approvingly if she'd heard her great-granddaughter saying to me and my siblings, "We'll see that you get a college education if you want one, otherwise we'll help you get a start. Then, you're on your own. Your father and I have our own plans."

Ickka seems to have had her own plans, as well. She had been bound to Jann by her parents. She was bound to her children by nature. All of this was mandated by God, and she had no quarrel with it. But God had taken Jann and, when her duty to her children was done, these matters were finished. She could then follow her own heart—God willing.

Whether she articulated her plan or not, with diligence and hard work, with saving and spending wisely, by utilizing best farming practices, she would expand her farming operations. Then as each of the boys married there would be farm acreage for them—not free, of course. No one ever appreciates anything that's free, but at a good price and terms and in exchange for the land and a quit claim on any future inheritance. She wanted no repeat of her experience with the State of Illinois.

What did Elsche Catharina think as she heard her mother's plans for her brothers? At sixteen she was a woman, capable of bearing children and caring for a home and a husband. But her mother needed her. Her brothers needed her. There was little Eilert with the energy of a young hellion who seemed daily to be in imminent danger of a catastrophic accident, of falling into fireplace or well. There was young Weert, his clothes seeming to find nails to rip on without human intercession. Who would keep the boys safe and their garments mended if she left?

No. She would have to continue as the family maid and caregiver until Gesche and Jenny were old enough to take her place. She would tend the young ones and do the cooking and feeding of animals and gardening. If she'd had her eye on a likely husband, if she'd been attracted to one of the handsome young men at church, her father's death meant the death, as well, of her hopes for an early marriage. There'd be no home of her own for her. Not now. Not for years to come.

And then? Would Elsche Catharina receive some return on this investment of time and energy in her siblings? Hardly. There was nothing in Ickka's plan for her or her sisters. No education, no farm, no relief from the endless work that had been Ickka's life. It'd always been this way for Ostfriesen women. They labored from dawn to dusk first in their father's home and then in their husband's. It was a woman's lot. It was mandated by God.

This might be the new world and elsewhere in it women might be calling for civil rights. Women certainly were marching in New York City. Women were going to college, even a few of them were becoming doctors. Soon the first women would get a vote in local elections, but these possibilities were not a local reality in South Prairie. If Elsche Catharina knew any of this or felt moments of rebellion or self-pity, she'd have received no sympathy. Here among the Ostfriesens, women were still chattel—tied to husband or father, to uncle or master.

Except in the Buss family something very strange had happened on a short-term basis. Ickka had bound Elsche Catharina not to a man but to herself.

Ickka had organized her own very quiet and private emancipation. She was bound to no one but herself and her children. So in 1859, Ickka turned away prospective suitors for herself and her oldest daughter and, with everyone in the family including two-year-old Eilert helping, began the process of expanding what we would now call an agricultural enterprise … doing it not by borrowing but by saving, by striking good deals, by growing more per acre and demanding fair prices, by skillfully determining when to plant and when to leave the land fallow, figuring which crops would grow best and where, by buying, selling, breeding, and butchering animals. In short she farmed using her brains and her own resources and working 24-7.

It's ironic. Ickka was the most conservative of women, but she knew what she wanted, and she knew she didn't need a husband to get it. So, she put one foot in front of the other, the way she always had, lowered her head and did what needed doing. She farmed well and saw that her sons did, too. That was her duty. She was beyond frugal in her lifestyle—never spent when she could trade, never traded when she could sell, and used and cared for what she had until it fell into tatters or rot. A luxury for Ickka remained what it always had been—an hour of rest during a church service.

So, she scrimped and saved and, then, the war came.

17
Implementing the Plan

For the first three years Ickka's plan worked and the little ones grew bigger and stronger. The war they'd feared began, but at first few in South Prairie let it affect them in any significant way. Yes. There were changes in the township as a whole as young 'English' men rushed to enlist, leaving women, boys, and old men to do the farming. In fact there was such an outpouring of volunteerism that the government couldn't arm or equip many thousands of the Illinois boys who lined up to serve. They were sent home.

The war fever even hit a group of Ostfriesen boys who'd emigrated to the Golden area—Albert Albers, Luppe Albers, Garrelt A. Garrells, John P. Huls and Ahlrich Park. Of course, everyone said it was the drink and maybe it was because they didn't understand English or it might've been the exciting sound of the recruiter's drummer and the mob's cheers. Whatever. The boys signed up as part of Company K of the 119th Illinois.

Four months later they were all captured in Tennessee. A year later Albert Albers was dead in a Confederate prison, and his body came home to Golden. Albert was dead, and the other boys had been paroled back to the Union and were sent to fight in one battle after another. Their letters of carnage, mindless marches, mud, lice, and butchery came at intervals as sobering reminders of why not to enlist.

So, things continued more or less in its usual pattern except for war news trumpeting Union defeats, with the lists of dead being posted in nearby towns, with grain sales at all-time highs, with the Union Army buying up as much beef as a farm could produce, with the mills of the North demanding more and more raw materials. For the Ostfriesens, their farms morphed into money machines—everything that went into the ground or came out of it was gold-plated.

At first getting produce to market wasn't easy. The war closed the Mississippi but turned the Port of Chicago into a booming enterprise.

"Thank God for the railroad," everyone said because South Prairie seed came in and grain went out by rail to Chicago and thence via ship out of the Port of Chicago, because South Prairie beef made it to the eastern cities and into Union bellies via the railroad, because corn from South Prairie farms reached the horses of the Union cavalry the same way.

At home Ickka drove hard bargains for her harvests, quietly amassing her dollars first in bundles of hundreds, then of thousands, converting what she could to gold and land. She spent more time in the village store during the winter months listening to talk about markets and how they worked, learning what she needed to know to strike ever more profitable deals. Heinrich did a man's labor. The younger boys, even, were all old enough to take up some of the burden.

Elsche Catharina, though, would have been increasingly restless with her lot and, in the third year of the war, she was finally allowed to say "I do" to Wilhelm Hinrichs Flesner, a twenty-three-year-old son of a neighboring family that Ickka knew well—in fact one day, far in the future, Ickka would marry Wilhelm's uncle.

While the Ostfriesen community celebrated Elsche Catharina and Wilhelm's wedding, the State of Illinois passed the Enrollment Act—it was a form of conscription, and no one was yet certain if it would affect unnaturalized aliens. If the State ignored the distinction between citizens and men who'd grown up in America but failed to officially regularize their status? Well, that didn't help Hinrich or Gerhard. Just a year before his death, their father had taken out citizenship, giving his offspring automatic citizenship. But Elsche Catharina's new husband and Janna's soon-to-be husband, Christopher Miller?

The Enrollment Act was the State's way of trying to meet Lincoln's demand for more troops, was necessary because no one, now, had the least intention of volunteering. In fact, the new law was met with resistance, both armed and passive.

The Ostfriesen men of South Prairie—those who'd taken out U.S. citizenship or declared an intention to do so—probably behaved much as men did throughout the state. They obtained medical exemptions, they bought surrogates as replacements, they claimed status as conscientious objectors, they left for the wild West or fled to Canada, they gave false names and obtained false papers. Many, including the Buss and Miller men, learned with relief that they were exempt for the time being because they could prove their status as unnaturalized aliens.

With this somber reality of war news and draft resistance as background to their happiness, Wilhelm Flesner and Elsche Catharina set up housekeeping on his 90-acre Adams County farm. The next year they marked the passage of time and the firm establishment of the Buss family in America by producing the first member of the third Ostfriesen-American generation in the person of a baby girl they named Lena Wilhelms.

Ickka was a grandmother, and there was another christening at the Emmanuel South Prairie Lutheran Church.

Such celebrations were welcomed in a world that seemed

to have gone crazy. The war had precipitated a slaughter unprecedented in human history, the war machine demanding more and more bodies, marching them onto the butcher's floor. In the end close to 700,000 would die. Around 1,100,000 names would clog the casualty lists.

Illinois, a state that had already given so many—more than almost any other northern state, was asked to send more and more. The Union Army's demand for troops was insatiable, but draft resistance had become an art. One practiced for the last time when conscription came back to the Fourth District and South Prairie. It was 1864, and it had even less effect on South Prairie and Golden than the previous efforts. In all of Adams County 3,579 names were pulled from the lottery pool but only 431 men marched off to war.

Ickka listened to talk of the killing fields while standing around Golden's potbelly stoves or sitting on neighbor's porches. After church, at weddings and funerals, she heard about wounded soldiers burning to death in the forests of the Wilderness and the blood-soaked ground of Spotsylvania. She would hold her meager purchases or eat a piece of cake and learn about the fights in the Shenandoah, about Washington, D.C. almost overrun, about Sherman's scorched earth march to the sea. She probably had little sympathy for the people of the South. If she knew her great granddaughter's favorite expression, "They made their beds, now they have to lie in them," she would no doubt have used it.

But it became more and more clear to her that the wholesale destruction of southern land and southern manpower would mean a continuing boom in northern agriculture for the foreseeable future—no matter whether the South surrendered or not.

She bought more land. She expanded her farming operation.

As for Gerhard, he could see that it was high time he married and branched off on his own. Working for his mother was a dead-end street. He'd never inherit the farm. Besides, who could tell what might happen next.

In that uncertain frame of mind and in that dreadful time, he went courting and brought home a wife, wedding Fentje (Fanny) Saltoff, another offspring of an Ostfriesen immigrant. Notably, before the marrying was done, three Saltoff girls would connect with Ickka's sons.

Also that same year, 1864, Jann's sister, Gesche Buss Franken—that indomitable pioneer and immigrant woman, died. Whatever Gesche and Ickka thought about each other during the early years of Ickka's marriage—the trials of the ocean crossing, the days together in Quincy, the tragedies of their first year in America—each of their shared experiences had formed a link in a very long chain that bound them closely together. Now, with Gesche dead, the last of the truly strong relationships that had connected Ickka to her Ostfriesen past were gone.

In such a short time, so much had changed. The prairie had completely disappeared from South Prairie. All the land that could be farmed, no matter how poor, was being farmed. Plattdeutsch was spoken throughout the area; Hochdeutsch was the language in church, and English was used in schools. The Ostfriesen work ethic and agricultural knowledge had filled the area with neat and tidy farms connected by arrow-straight roads—the by-ways—that had replaced canals in their lives. Golden was a work in progress with a promising future. There were churches and schools, a grain mill, grocery stores, a lunch counter, a barber shop, and a bank. It was no longer necessary to go all the way to Quincy for medical help or legal advice.

Most of all, a new generation had grown up.

Anyone could see it. All you had to do was look as the Buss family gathered at Emmanuel South Prairie Lutheran for Gesche's funeral service. Despite the deaths, there were ten of them now. As the pastor spoke words of consolation, Ickka could likely get glimpses of the future, of the day sometime soon when her offspring would all be married and their children would be filling the church. But before she moved over to make room for them, she had a lot of work to do. Besides, she had a life of her own to live.

18
Endowing the Offspring—1860's

The war ended. Peace descended and the Mississippi reopened to traffic, but the war had changed the way people did things. The high prices for agricultural products that had prevailed during the war didn't drop, as Ickka had expected, while the boom in railroad construction meant more competition, more routes, and lower costs. Ickka was able to buy even more land now. And she did, fulfilling her promise to her oldest son and deeding over eighty acres of developed farmland to Gerhard and Fanny in exchange for a modest $3,200. A year later Ickka signed over land valued at an additional $1,600 to the couple in exchange for a quit claim on her estate.

Gerhard had been launched. He was out of the nest and on his own, but Ickka had four more sons to go. That meant she just had to work harder. She needed a lot of land.

In the meantime tragedy returned to South Prairie. Ickka's youngest daughter, Gesche, died at the age of twelve. More than the loss of her husband, more than the loss of her sister-in-law and friend, this blow from God laid Ickka low. Twice now God had taken a daughter. They hadn't been babies. They'd been people with personalities and characters. They'd made places for themselves in the hearts of everyone but most of all in the heart of their mother.

A very pregnant Elsche Catharina came to help. The ladies of Emmanuel Lutheran gathered, bringing covered dishes, staying to console with their presence. Gesche's friends from church gathered as much to seek consolation as to give it. As for Ickka, Ostfriesen customs meant there was never time to sit and mope. Her house was full of people who'd come to console. What they did was to make more mouths that needed feeding. Mud came in with their feet, and it had to be cleaned. They needed heat, so the fire had to be fed. They ate the food they bought and then some. So she and Elsche Catharina cooked, used up stores of preserved foods, cut wood and still had to tend their livestock and the never-ending farm chores.

But that was all to the good. Ickka and Gesche's siblings got through the funeral and the period of grieving by the grace of custom and work. There was always so much to do. Always there was so much to do, especially once Elsche Catharina returned to her own home. That left only little Janna to help in the house. At least they could get back to something like normal.

Except sorrow was not done with the Buss family. The pregnant girls, Elsche Catharina and Gerdhard's wife, Fentje, both lost their baby boys at birth—sons they named Johann. Ickka sat in the church at the infants' funerals, most likely holding back her tears, praying for the tiny souls of her grandsons. Their deaths, at least, were what happened in the normal course of events. She consoled herself with the thought. You can hope infants won't die, but often they do. Hadn't she lost her first born? Didn't she know all the platitudes about God taking those he loved most and didn't she know all the words? Infant death happened. It was to be expected. So why did she feel like she was the one who had lost yet another child?

Grief gave way the next year to a red-letter event. Ickka had the sublime pleasure of seeing her first granddaughter, Wilhelmina Catharina, graduate from the first confirmation class at Emanuel South Prairie Lutheran. As she sat in her pew surrounded by friends and relatives, she would have been near enough to the altar to smell the candle wax and the slightly musty smell of the pastor's robes. She would've turned her head with everyone else to watch the teen-aged boys in their suits and the girls in their white confirmation dresses come down the center aisle that divided the men's seating area from the women's. And she might've shaken her head over the unnecessary expense of Wilhelmina Catharina's dress. She'd neither had nor expected a special dress for her own confirmation.

But she would've smiled, anyway. Partly because the children looked so lovely. Mostly because the ceremony showed how her church had grown from that first Sunday in 1848 when she'd opened the door of her cabin to Gesche Franken and her daughter. Or, when they brought the stricken Franken boys home and had gathered together with their neighbors, the Westphalian couples, to worship and mourn. That day, sitting on benches and beds, they'd prayed together, reading scripture from the one book they'd brought to America—a Bible. Twenty years ago that had been with a wilderness untouched by man outside the door. It'd been twenty years almost to the day, but to Ickka it probably seemed like yesterday. Hard to believe so much time had passed even when she considered how much had happened.

But what she needed now was a grandson, and in 1868 Elsche Catharina gave her one. Ickka went to church for the christening and to accept the congratulations of the entire community and to thank the good Lord for repeating history in a positive way. If He was going to deal out the bad, at least He was equal handed and gave the good, too. Just as Gerhard had been healthy, so was this boy they called Heinrich Wilhelm Flesner.

Ickka was less pleased and felt less comfortable within the

community when Janna decided she wanted to marry that bright young man, Chris Miller. He was five years older than the girl, a fact Ickka had probably been quick to note. This wasn't a problem except that Janna was only sixteen. "Wait," she'd counseled, most likely knowing it wasn't so much the age thing that bothered her as the loss of the last of her household helpers. Gesche was dead, and her plan would have called for the labor of each girl until they were at least eighteen.

She still had the four boys to feed and who would do the cooking and the other household chores if Janna left?

But sixteen was considered a good age to marry. Chris was in a position to care for a wife and children. He already owned his own farm, thanks to his father and to his own profitable land speculations. Then, too, marriage was a holy sacrament and a religious obligation. No. If Ickka pressed her objections, she would've done so in the face of church and community values, not to mention inviting attention to another matter.

People might well have reacted with: "Sure Moder Buss needs help at home. Those boys are a handful. And, haven't we been saying this all along? Isn't it time she gave those boys a father and for her to return to the work God meant a woman to do."

So, no matter how she really felt, she would have smiled and exerted herself to be pleasant as Chris and Janna spoke their vows in their pastor's living room, which is where he conducted wedding services. She must have cooked the traditional foods and helped decorate the church for the wedding reception. She must have exchanged polite phrases with Bertha Miller, the groom's mother. She certainly gave the young couple gifts, maybe a choice ram from her herd of sheep or a few chickens so Janna could start a flock of her own. And that was that! Her last daughter was gone.

Births, marriages, and deaths had always been the core events in Ickka's life, but usually these had been other people's births, marriages, and deaths. More and more, they concerned her personally. They seemed to come in rapid succession, every month or so she was in church for a christening or a funeral or a marriage, each year presented multiple reasons to celebrate and grieve.

Through it all, Ickka continued farming and buying land but seeing the day when she would escape the burden of responsibility coming closer and closer.

19
Little Janna, Better Known as Jenny

By the time her mother died, Jenny probably was proud of her and of being her daughter. It's not so clear she'd felt the same way as a child for, as far back as she could remember, Ickka kept Jenny hard at work. As soon as she could walk, she'd had daily chores. It was: "Janna, fetch water from the well." Or, "Why is the woodbox empty?" Or, "Get out and feed the chickens." And, "Take those scraps to the pigs." Her days were crammed with responsibility … bone-breaking, fatiguing responsibilities that never diminished, just became more onerous.

At least she'd had help. Her big sister Elsche Catharina was always there to show her an easier way to do something or to teach her to pick up a dropped stitch in her knitting. Or, as sisters will, to nag her and swat her for real or imagined delinquencies. And she had her baby sister, Gesche, who was just a year younger and, most likely, her very best friend.

Then, Elsche Catharina got married. At the age of eleven, Jenny became the boss of the house and all it contained—at least whenever her mother wasn't in it, which meant most of the daylight hours. For a time Gesche was always there to help her, and it wasn't too bad. But then Gesche died. With her passing Jenny lost a companion and helper. But at least some of the chores they'd shared had gone away. Eilert was eight and Weert was ten the year of Gesche's death, so both were out of the house and out from under foot during the day. Plus, Eilert and Weert could tend the chickens and hogs, could throw hay to the larger animals and do the milking plus whatever tasks their Moder set for them.

That left Jenny with all the cooking and scrubbing and mending and cleaning. It left Jenny as the only girl in a family of boys. It was just Jenny feeding wood into the stove, stirring stews, tending chickens, weeding the garden, man-handling a paddle to move dirty farm clothes around in boiling water and lye. She carded wool, herded geese and cows, rendered fat, butchered chickens, and preserved fruits and vegetables. In the evening it would be Jenny and her mother with heads or backs bent over their sewing, darning, knitting, or ironing. The boys had their books. Jenny had beans to snap, peas to shell, corn to husk, onions to weave into garlands.

For sixteen years little Jenny had lived a life barely different than her mother's childhood in Ostfriesland. Just as her mother had been, she was a servant in her own home. Just as her mother's, her world was severely limed by the close walls of a cabin. Her social life would be limited to Sunday outings to church and occasional walks to visit with her big sister. Her luxuries would have consisted of one good dress for church plus, most likely, a ribbon or two for her hair. What schooling she'd received had ended when her presence at home became essential.

Her older brothers, raised in Ostfriesen traditions, would have looked on her as of little value. One of these boys, Heinrich, is remembered for domestic violence, a behavior common in the old country and one he probably learned at his father's knee. Did he exercise the flat of his hand or use his fists on his little sister? Well. It seems a safe enough assumption. And, if Heinrich practiced such abuse, what about the other boys? It's hard to say. We know enough about Weert, who was to marry a Miller girl, to be sure that wasn't true in his case. But the rest? In any event,

Jenny could not be said to have had a happy childhood.

Yet, her youth was a period of transition for the Buss family, and she was in an ideal position to observe the changes. The older boys—Gerhard, Heinrich, and Johann (Jenny called him John)—adhered to the old customs. Not that they weren't open to better farming practices, but they were married to a business model set up long centuries in the past. The younger boys felt no such tie. Weert, for one, had definitely inherited the merchant gene from the Buss family line. He was brilliant with numbers and had an instinct for negotiating and bargaining. As for baby Eilert, he was fascinated with the exploding technology of the late nineteenth century. Yet, the entire family was tied to a piece of rural America that their parents and fellow countrymen had tried to make as much like their homeland as possible. So, all of them to one degree or another were heavily influence by old traditions and thought patterns.

Among other things, this means that Ickka gave her sons their love of the land and their belief that land and prosperity went together. Ickka taught both sons and daughters that all wealth is derived from the land and that economic theories of unrelated services generating money were so much nonsense. Ickka was as tight an agrarian fiscal conservative as a person could be.

She'd been a liberal in one sense only—feminism. Not that she would have seen herself as a feminist or as a liberal (if she'd known the word). The division of her resources among her sons and her consignment of her daughters to marriage was proof of that. But Ickka had to have considered her own life and how she lived it as an exception to the general rule.

Still, one exception begets another. Why didn't her daughters show the same determination and drive and grab at the same 'exceptions'? Why didn't they demand the right to keep some of the egg money generated by their efforts or the right to pocket profits from the wool they carded and spun. Didn't their brothers get to keep the small sums they earned from their own projects? And, why didn't the girls ask for the right to buy land from their mother at cost as their brothers did? Finally, why did they meekly drop out of school?

In fact many women of their generation were doing a great deal more than seeking an education and a share of the family business. They were going west to find land and to farm, were knocking on college doors, moving into retailing jobs, writing books, exploring the world by themselves. They were employed as journalists and commercial artists, owned their own businesses and even disguised themselves and served in the military.

Jenny and Elsche Catharina could certainly see that a woman could be as strong and capable as a man. They just had to look at their mother. A woman could manage her own accounts. A woman could sell her own crops and buy her own land. A woman could make a good trade and a good living without a husband or father to "look after" her. Their mother showed them exactly that. Yet, both her girls moved from Ickka's domination to a husband's, perhaps because Ickka raised them to do just that.

It's likely, though, there was another influence at work on the teen-aged Jenny. Peer-group and societal pressure. While the radio and television, the telephone and internet had yet to homogenize the world, Golden was not indifferent to national trends. They had newspapers and magazines, the latter providing a romanticized idea of what girls could/should do and how their lives would revolve around their marriages. Magazines like *Godey's Ladies Magazine*, a monthly that came into the Miller store in Golden and was passed around from hand to hand, were avidly read. Fashions portrayed in its pages were replicated on sewing machines, knitting patterns copied out in laborious script, recipes adapted to available ingredients. On its pages, too, girls like Jenny could avidly examine the latest in cooking appliances and yearn to own their own. Think of it! Cooking on coal. And, what would happen next? Not just a hand pump in the kitchen but a water closet for bathing?

The girls had spent their childhood hearing echoes of community chatter about their mother being "different." She might be admired, but she never was "quite one of us." Likely, the girls had been teased and mocked and mortified. As children, they'd been caught between two forces, helpless to change their situation. As adults, though, they could prove themselves 'normal,' could transform their status and become conforming members of society. And, what a wonderful and rewarding society it was.

So when Chris Miller came courting and proposed, Jenny accepted. Marriage with only one man to look after would definitely mean a vast, an incredible improvement in her life, even if it did not open the glamorous world she'd mooned over in *Godey's*. Still, she wouldn't be marrying just any old farm boy. Although only nineteen, Chris had taken advantage of the commercial opportunities offered by the Civil War and had already established himself as a man in the community. By 1866, when Golden was platted, he was able to handle the financing to buy a block of town lots which is still marked on the official plat with his name.

So, Jenny escaped home through marriage and moved into her own house. A real house, not a cabin, and on land Chris had bought from his father for $4,000.

It certainly wasn't luxurious, but this first house would have had a kitchen where Chris and Jenny ate their meals, one perhaps with the latest in cast iron stoves that sported a well for heating water and produced heat for the kitchen as well as fueling an oven and top burners for cooking. Such a stove would have been a huge step up from the old wood-burning stove Jenny had spent her life nursing.

Even so, every six days the new contraption used an average of 292 pounds of coal and 14 pounds of kindling. All of this had to be carried into the house and shoveled into a fire compartment that used 20 pounds of fuel per meal. In exchange the stove then produced over a six-day period 27 pounds of ash that had to be scraped out and disposed outside. The fact that this was seen as a huge improvement on the pre-Civil War kitchen stoves puts Jenny's work as a wife in perspective.

The house would also have a parlor and, probably, two bedrooms complete with real beds. Later in life we know Jenny kept a tin tub for bathing in her bedroom, and she may have done so at this point, as well. What a change from the sponge baths at home! Total immersion in hot water that no one had dirtied. Still, Jenny would still have had to haul water from the pump behind the back door to the stove and, then, from the stove in the kitchen to the bedroom.

Jenny had little time left over, certainly not time to hitch up a horse and drive into town to visit with other ladies. She still had relentless labor from dawn to long after winter nights set in, but she was almost immediately pregnant, and she seems to have been happy. There was only one man to keep fed and in clothes and no one to take away the results of her labor. The chickens she tended were hers. The eggs they produced were sold to her father-in-law to retail in his store, the money put away in a coffee can. The milk she wrung from her cow and separated and churned produced more income besides going into great cakes and breads that Chris loved and, we can assume, praised.

In fact he seems to have been a devoted husband, appreciative of the way she could season a roast and find new recipes and sew a perfect seam. He may have brought home gifts of pretty cotton fabrics so she could stitch herself new dresses and might even have agreed when she wanted to buy a ready-to-wear coat out of a catalog.

Through it all, Chris grew more prosperous, bought more land and acquired stature in the community. So, the years went by and the children came. Lena was the first.

"Space them out," Ickka or one of the other women would have told her, explaining how to satisfy her husband without producing a child. Ostfriesen women, as we have seen, believed children should come every two years and not earlier. Mary was born two years after Lena. Ida followed two years later. Five years of marriage had brought Chris and Janna three little girls who might well have been spoiled by their Miller grandparents. But that would not have been Ickka's way. Finally, in the same year that Ickka married Heinrich Flessner, Janna had a boy who was named after his Miller grandfather and his father. Hermann Christoph Miller had entered the world.

With the addition of yet another baby, the farmhouse was beginning to seem cramped.

At this point Chris had begun traveling up to Chicago on a regular basis to do business and to speculate in the grain market. Why not build a house more or less centrally located in Golden and near the train station? Besides Lena would soon be starting school, and she was much too little to be walking all that way. Chris acted on the thought and built a handsome home for his growing family, one that included all the new gadgets that had been appearing on the market and incorporated such luxuries as a butler's pantry, a formal parlor and a back parlor. Then, he went shopping and filled his new house with golden oak furniture and marble-top tables. The master bedroom was on the ground floor; children's bedrooms were on the second floor.

With the move into this establishment Jenny completed her transformation from farm drudge, and she couldn't scramble into this new life fast enough. She still worked from dawn to dark, but now she had help, and she no longer had farm chores. Lena started school. Jenny and Chris became members of the Emmanuel (Golden) Lutheran Church. Jenny, who was related in one way or another to many of the church congregation and to the parents of Lena's new school friends, was now living in close enough proximity to socialize regularly with them.

For the first time she could indulge in close friendships with other women, could participate in the daily activities of church and town. Also, her in-laws were nearby, her father-in-law having built a new two-story brick store in Golden during the same year she and Chris were married. Jenny could walk the few blocks to have tea with her mother-in-law and her two sisters-in-law. She could stroll down to the Miller's General Mercantile to pick up a spool of thread or to select a skein of yarn for a baby afghan or a sweater.

Bertha was born two years later. The Millers now had four girls—two of them in school—and a boy. It was a fine-sized family for this new generation of Americans, and Jenny was inclined to stop there. The house was full enough, and they'd yet to lose a baby unlike both her sister and oldest brother who between them had seen four of their babies die.

The next year brought one of the high points of Jenny's life in Golden. Her little brother, Weert, had moved into Golden when he was nineteen where he'd probably stayed with Jenny and Chris while clerking in the local stores, saving his money, and learning about trade. He'd also started courting Volkea Emminga, the beautiful daughter of Golden's leading citizen— and the man who'd brought the wind-driven grist mill to Golden.

Volkea and Weert

In 1878, Volkea said "yes," her father gave his approval, and her mother made Volkea's marriage the social event of the decade. As the groom's only sister, Jenny played a prominent role in the festivities.

Weert prospered and built a big lumber yard plus a brick office building. The senior Millers decided to retire from merchandising and to move back to Quincy where there were more amenities. Brother Gerhard lost his lovely wife, Fentje Saathoff Buss, and two months later married his hired help, Anna Flesner, who'd stepped in to care for the children. Chris bought more land and John Henry was born, christened Johann Heinrich. Little Hermann Christoph started school, Jenny's youngest brother, Eilert, married a Franzen girl, and Gerhard had another daughter. At home, young Mary showed signs of becoming a scholar while Hermann was having trouble learning his alphabet.

The year baby Bertha started school Jenny had yet another child. In 1882 Bernhard "Barney" Elic Miller joined the family. "This is definitely it," Jenny may have said. "We have four girls and three boys. Enough is enough."

Except life happens. Jenny's last surviving sister, Elsche Catharina, died. More babies were born to the brothers and some died; Chris bought more land.

Brother Johann, too, lost his wife and remarried eleven months later … "He waited a decent period," people said, and Chris and Jenny's young daughter, Bertha, was showing an artistic flair. Hermann Christoph hated school. Lena and Maria were top of their respective classes and, even though girls of their ages were normally thinking of marriage, both were talking about college. And Barney was approaching school age.

All of Jenny's children would be in school.

"It'll be lonely without a baby in the house," Jenny may have thought. Perhaps the idea of days of quiet persuaded her to begin another family. Perhaps, not. But one way or another, Gesina Maria Miller appeared in 1887, but not before the Miller-Buss branch of the family expanded in a very unexpected way.

20
Weert

Weert's enterprises prospered in these years, and he did more building, notably erecting a beautiful big house for his family that outshone every other Golden home except for that of his Emminga in-laws. Their enjoyment of it, however, was short-lived. The lovely Volkea, who everyone called Kate, died in 1886, leaving Weert with two babies, a big house that he and Kate had planned to fill with children, and more responsibility than he quite knew how to handle.

He went courting, and seven months later he remarried, the ceremony taking place at Immanuel Lutheran in Golden. The bride was a teenager from Quincy.

She was also a granddaughter of Bertha and Hermann Miller, a girl named Bertha Tansmann.

To tell this story, we need to go back in time to the Old Mill House and the birth of Behrendji's second child, Helene "Lena" Miller, a lovely little girl who entered the world during the reign of the three women—Behrendji, her mother-in-law, and sister-in-law. She'd emigrated with her parents, had gone to Quincy and then Golden with them before meeting and marrying a man from Lower Saxony. Frederick Tansmann was a suitable match for the daughter of a merchant, being one himself.

How he got that way, though, is a thoroughly American story. Frederick had no inherited wealth, had emigrated to America to win his fortune, and had seen the 1849 Gold Rush as his chance. It had been. He'd not only been among the rare few who actually found gold, he'd been one of the handful who'd put it to good use, joining the German community in Quincy. Fourteen years later when he met and married Lena, he was the owner of grocery/general store and had interests in diverse other businesses.

Lena, having been raised in a merchant's home, became an active participant in his affairs, helping with the store and a saloon and bearing first a son, then a daughter, Bertha. Tragically, the tall, willowy mother died six months later. Shortly thereafter, following the customs of the day, Frederick found and married another attractive woman from a prominent and well-to-do Quincy family, Friedricke Ruff. Together they had three more children, raising them plus Lena's two in a large and socially active home.

With a stepmother who was prominent in the Ladies Social Union and a father who was active as, among other things, a Mason, Bertha went through the Quincy school system. She'd just graduated from high school and gone to work in a local millenary shop (probably the one owned by her Aunt Mary … her mother's sister) when she met Weert while he was in Quincy on a business trip.

Weert needed a mother for his two young children. But Bertha? She'd inherited $1,000 (approximate $29,000 in today's money) from her grandfather Hermann Miller a few years earlier, was earning her own way, and had a father and step-mother who were more than well-off. Weert not only came encumbered by children but was fourteen years older. On the other hand, he was a handsome and a considerate man, was a brother to Bertha's gentle and loving Aunt Jenny, and was part of her own Ostfriesen heritage. More, as a practical consideration, Bertha could expect marriage to give her a leading role in Golden's Ostfriesen society.

She said a resounding "yes" and talked her parents into agreeing.

When they walked down the aisle at Immanuel Lutheran, even Kate Emminga's best friends had to agree that Weert had brought home a good mother for Kate's children. Most of all, people began to think it was a love match, as well, one that lasted 44 years.

Change

It was Chris who really changed everything for Jenny. He had a habit of dickering, of speculation. He'd purchased empty lots in Golden against the kind of growth the town was experiencing. He bought acreages in the countryside to lease and resell. He bought grain futures and any other futures he thought promising, depending on the year.

Jenny probably paid little attention until one day he announced he'd purchased a farm in Kinderhook, a long day's buggy drive from Golden. He might well have come back with pictures to show her.

Kodak had recently created a camera that the average person could use. All you did was aim it and push a button. When the pre-loaded film was completely used, you sent the whole camera back to the factory for film development and, eventually, a stack of pictures came in the mail along with the reloaded camera. The ease of creating pictures captivated everyone. As for the land … ? Well. Jenny could see for herself.

The men of the family gathered to talk about Chris' new venture and to question his wisdom. "Yes," he would have agreed with them. The land was prone to flooding, the river washing away the good topsoil, but hadn't their fathers had to drain the

South Prairie lands? Hadn't they dealt with the North Sea? The Mississippi might be big, but it was nothing compared to the Sea. Anyway, he'd figured out a way to divert the flood waters and to drain them off while holding onto his own soil and capturing the rich sediment brought by the river.

In fact he would successfully adapt techniques from the old country. The flood waters of the Mississippi's Hadley Creek drainage could prove a gold mine for him. It did. The gates he built to channel water worked and his system remained in use for over a hundred years. It ended only because the great Mississippi flood of 1993 finally carried the old and deteriorating system away.

But that was the future. Right now Chris was in the planning phase and right now he intended for the whole family to move to Kinderhook. Jenny was—quite understandably—aghast.

Chris, her husband, expected her to leave her beautiful house where she'd borne him five children, to abandon sewing parties and friends, to give up her church activities and committees and good works—leave behind everything she loved. And the children? All their friends were here. All their cousins and aunts and uncles lived nearby. Why, she knew every house and building on every block in the town, could tell you when it was built, who had lived in it, who'd been married or died in it, and any other significant event that had occurred in or around it.

Chris wanted her to leave her home, her people, and her memories and live in the wilderness of Pike County? *Wither thou goest,* the Bible said, but surely God didn't intend her to go to Kinderhook. Was there even a Lutheran church there? Worse. They wouldn't be living in the tiny village of Kinderhook but out on a farm! She remembered farm life, and she wanted no part of it … ever again.

Jenny said 'no.' She said, "No. No. No." She certainly used passive resistance on a major scale.

For a time, Chris commuted back and forth. Jenny gave no sign of moderating her position. Finally, Chris hit on a solution of sorts, on a way to ease the transition for his wife. He built an exact replica of their Golden house on the Kinderhook property, complete with a butler's pantry. Such conceit might make him a laughing stock among his new neighbors, but he did it. He laid out the yard so she could have the phlox she loved along the walk that led to the front door. He made improvements. The kitchen had an updated store and a water pump right next to the sink.

In a farm culture that prided itself on its splendid barns, manicured fields, and glossy animals, one that considered money spent on house and grounds to be wasted, the tale of Jenny's house, one assumes, never lost in the retelling. A butler's pantry in a farm house? Imagine!

"Well!" people said. "For lands sake! Lawdy lawdy! Will the world of wonders never cease. What is that man Chris Miller thinking! He must be made of money to squander it so."

Maybe so. But the house accomplished its purpose. Jenny recognized when she'd been defeated. She packed up her children, saw her furniture loaded carefully onto wagons along with trunks and boxes carrying blankets and clothing, pottery and china, flatware and serving utensils, toys and family memorabilia. And one sunny day she walked past the phlox on her front walkway for the last time, climbed up to the seat of her buggy, accepted one-year-old Sena who was passed up to sit beside her, and set out on the long drive to Kinderhook.

As Chris had said, it was beautiful there on the rich Mississippi floodplain bordered as the farm was on two sides by steep wooded bluffs. Nearby was the village of Kinderhook which seemed to spill downwards off the heights, only hints of houses peeking through a forest of green until, at the foot of the bluff, the trees thinned and you could see white buildings spread out around a church steeple. What could be more restful to the eyes.

A levee protected town and land, and a railway line led to Hannibal across the river. You could change trains there for one that went up river to Quincy. Or you could take the east-bound train to Jacksonville where the tracks met a line running north to Chicago. Vegetation thrived. So did every kind of insect, but Chris had purchased woven wire sheets, attached them to frames and set them into doors and windows. The "screens" didn't keep the bugs out, but they certainly helped.

It really was pretty there. From her second floor windows looking west, Jenny could see the green and white Mississippi bluffs to the south of Hannibal, their limestone faces brilliant on a clear day. To her east and north the curving line of tree-covered cliffs rose into the blue sky, hiding the flat prairielands of her childhood. The views were lovely, but for a girl raised with far horizons it might well have seemed claustrophobic. It was as different from Golden as a white rose from a red one. It smelled differently, too. An ubiquitous damp, earthy odor underlay everything. No perfume could long mask it. No delicious cooking smells prevented it from invading her kitchen. But, soon, she stopped noticing.

The railway line was a prime feature of Kinderhook, and there was a train station in the nearby village of Hull. Best of all, Chris' twin brothers both lived in close proximity, one owning the grain elevator, the other with a 400-acre farm. From Hull, Chris could cheaply ship goods both east and west, and with a transit in Springfield his crops had an easy trip north to Chicago. Likewise, an overnight on the train took Chris himself to the Chicago markets where he could spend the day in business, then home again in a comfortable Pullman bed. As for Jenny, she could take the train to Jacksonville to visit her children—the ones that lived there during the school year. Or she could go west across the river into Hannibal, change there for a forty-minute trip to Quincy where Chris's mother, Bertha Miller, now lived with her oldest daughter Mary (Hermann having died a few years earlier). Yes. In a period of unpaved or no roads, the train was a great luxury.

And, so, they continued to prosper. The challenge, often, was getting into Hull or Kinderhook. Chris owned a fine buggy with excellent springs, which helped. As long as the weather wasn't too wet, getting to town was a matter first of catching the horse, bringing him into the barn, putting him into harness and hooking him to the buggy. Usually the family used one of the big tractable farm horses, and this hitching-up process took less than half an hour. On the other hand, the work animals seldom could be persuaded to do more than walk, meaning it was faster to simply rely on your own two legs.

Once she'd moved, Jenny tried to keep her life intact and as unchanged as possible. Her lovely furniture, of course, went with her. She had a fine oak dining room table that would seat twelve with ease. Her piano took its place of honor in the front parlor and a spinning wheel and a quilting frame were installed in the back parlor. She had a linen press for sheets and blankets, tablecloths, lengths of fabric, boxes of yarn, and spare doilies. She filled her butler's pantry shelves with her good china. Her flatware went into drawers, and she found places for her silver tea service and her perky little chocolate set a pot and matching demitasse-sized cups. The heavier pottery intended for daily use stayed in the kitchen along with her iron kettles and pans and a fine set of copper molds.

Among Jenny's other possessions was a massive black walnut bed, its carved headboard taller than most men. Bertha had brought it with her from Germany and had given it to the newlyweds as a wedding present. It plus a tin bathing tub, a fine tall chest of drawers, and an oak wardrobe took up almost every bit of space in the bedroom.

As she had, even in Golden, Jenny planted a garden. She'd always fed her family through the winter on her own vegetables grown in her own garden, and she attributed the good health of her children in large measure to the nourishing effects of carefully preserved garden produce. Now she also had an orchard, which gave her fresh fruits and more of her own produce to bottle or dry. Then, there were the animals. She had her chickens, and they kept a cow. Jenny had a special affection for pigs, raising a few piglets each summer to turn into hams and bacons come fall.

Summers, of course, were busy times on the Kinderhook farm and not just because of the crops, harvesting, food preservation, and livestock cycles. Summers were when the children all assembled. Chris and Jenny's growing brood gathered and were joined by a multitude of cousins. As mentioned above, Chris' brother Bernard (Barney) Miller with his wife, Altje, lived in nearby Hull where they had a total of five children over a period roughly similar to Chris and Jenny's childbearing years. Barney's twin brother, Eilert Hermann, was there as well, with his wife Henrietta and their eight children. Like the others, Hermann's children came at intervals—the first born at the same time as Jenny's second in 1871, the last being the same age as Walter (Chris and Jenny's second to last). Taken all together between the three brothers, there were twenty-three children and various and sundry grandchildren in one stage of development or another over the fifty-year period that the Millers lived in Pike County.

Another factor that played in Jenny's mothering and life in Kinderhook was age. Her childbearing phases produced two distinct generations among her offspring. The first seven had come along at two-year intervals. The second group started after a gap of five years. Perhaps because of this the last three had little in common with the earlier Miller children and, in time, drifted off to form a sub-family of their own. This would prove important in the long run and will be discussed later.

In the meantime, the move from Golden to Kinderhook had another unintended consequence. It separated Jenny and her younger offspring from their Ostfriesen heritage and effectively removed them from Golden's Ostfriesen colony. Raised, just as her mother had been and in a rigidly structured home, Jenny may have felt this change more than the others. Nevertheless, surrounded by children and family and busy as she was from dawn to long past dark with the same chores that had formed the pattern of her early life, it's doubtful that she had trouble adapting. She did more shopping in Jacksonville than she would've thought possible, and she went home to Golden for major events—like her oldest daughter, Lena, marrying an Adams County boy in 1891. As for language, she continued to speak Plattdeutsch in her home, read her Bible in Hochdeutsch, and use English when necessary, the occasions becoming more frequent as she aged, English taking over as the language of the church liturgy and being the only language spoken by her younger grandchildren.

That marriage of Lena's. Jenny was probably more than a little relieved when Lena announced she would marry the Brenneman boy ... not that he was a boy but a graduate of the Illinois College who was practicing medicine in Chicago. Yes. He'd make a good husband for her oldest daughter. Lena would settle down and lead a normal life.

Which would be a great change for the better. For a long, long time now, when Jenny looked at Lena and her other older daughters, she probably felt rather like the hen who'd hatched out goose eggs. The girls just didn't fall into the Golden/Ostfriesen pattern. Like Ickka before her, Jenny and her cousins and friends had learned their letters and numbers ... acquired a little reading; a little figuring. That was all a girl needed to know. Everyone said so. As for Chris, he hadn't been much more interested in schooling than the other boys of his acquaintance.

So where did they get these intellectual and accomplished young women? Well. Jenny knew the answer to that. The fault lay with Bertha Miller and Chris' sisters. They'd encouraged Lena and her sisters to be different. As for Chris, he was just as bad. He'd moved into the wider world with his forays into the realms of higher finance. He was welcome in the Chicago and New York homes of his colleagues on the Boards of Trade. He'd traveled to Europe not only to visit his ancestral home but to tour the European capitals. He'd learned to admire the many beautiful and accomplished women he'd met, and he saw no reason his daughters couldn't grow up with the skills that would allow them to move in the same society.

Thus, Lena and his other girls had an excellent education and were equipped to move through the larger American society and to be something other than farm wives. Yet? It must have been hard for Jenny to go against tradition, to see her daughters turn their backs on the hard life she'd endured, to set aside the old ways. Wasn't it just those things that had made her what she was? And wasn't what had been good for her, good for her daughters?

At some level, too, Jenny would have seen her daughters emulating their grandmother Ickka in their determination to conform just so far as necessary while still going their own way. Jenny had chosen the traditional role. Her daughters were another matter. They would marry and have families as Ickka had, but they would also exercise their individual talents and develop their own skills. This made Chris happy and proud. This made Jenny wonder. It hadn't been her way, but what could you expect in this "modern" world!

Jenny would have been only marginally aware that there'd been a revolution in American education since her own youth.

In the year she married Chris there were only about 160 high schools in the entire country. A decade later the figure had grown to almost 800, when the census of 1880 showed that ... shockingly ... the proportion of literacy in young women was higher than that in young men.

Oberlin College had been the first to admit women in 1837 and the University of Michigan accepted women in 1870. Illinois College in Jacksonville—the closest college to Golden—did not. Not yet.

In the event, Chris probably thought it all a fine idea when his oldest daughter announced that she'd applied for and been accepted at Illinois College pending a letter of approval and declaration of financial support from the father. Lena wanted to continue her schooling. She wanted to be a school teacher herself. She'd always done well in school, graduating with honors from her Jacksonville high school, and she thought it a good plan to obtain some practical use from her education. With a teaching certificate from a college, she could teach almost anywhere.

Thus, Jenny saw Lena married with a sense of relief. Her daughter was reverting to type, after all. She certainly would've loved the fact that Lena chose to be married in Golden among all of their relatives and friends. Afterwards, the two young people would leave on their wedding trip before settling first in Chicago and later moving to California.

Jenny's next major visits to Golden were sad ones. First came her brother Gerd's funeral in 1894. Then, her stepfather, Heinrich Flessner died and was buried the following year. And, like her mother before her, Jenny was learning that the red-letter events in her life would come faster and faster as she aged. The same year her step-father died, her third daughter, Ida, was married in Golden to a friend of her childhood. By this time, Illinois College had officially decided to accept women, and Mary had graduated with high marks. Like Lena, she'd then taught school for a time. Mary, however, did not find a beau or if she did she didn't keep him. Instead, she pleased her mother by returning to Kinderhook to help raise and educate her younger siblings.

There were other changes in that decade. Chris and his sister, Mary, who had lost her husband and now owned a hat shop in Quincy, made their first trip of many back to Ostfriesland and returned with glowing reports about their many cousins. Bertha Miller came to live on the Kinderhook farm, her help invaluable that year when Walter was born and four years later when Elmer William (my grandfather) came along as the last of Jenny's children. That was 1894.

"Willy," as she called the baby, was definitely the last. Jenny was finished with babies.

Ikke and Heinrich Flessner

21
A New Marriage

Sixteen years after Jann's death, the year Eilert turned eighteen and came of age, Ickka relaxed her iron grip on destiny, bowed gracefully to custom (since we can assume in this instance that custom and her wishes coincided), and remarried. Her new husband was another Ostfriesen, of course, a childhood friend by one account and a long-standing friend and neighbor by all. Heinrich Mimke Flessner was a widower with eight grown children of his own and a prosperous eighty-acre farm. If this wasn't a love match, it was the next best thing. The two were as compatible as two people can be, sharing friends, church, experiences, and life philosophies. He accepted Ickka as an independent woman. She accepted him as her companion and, in all likelihood, a lover. They both said their, "I do's," in Hochdeutsch.

What changed after the wedding? Ickka moved in with Heinrich, leaving her cabin behind—a big step for her. That said, she continued farming her own land with help from Eilert and hired men, not retiring until seven years later, in 1882. After all, she still had promises to her two youngest boys to fulfill.

The marriage doubled the size of her family, and every member of it still lived in the South Prairie/Golden area. Most of them also attended the Emmanuel South Prairie Lutheran Church although those with property close to Golden or in Golden, itself, had switched their attendance to the Emmanuel (Golden) Lutheran Church, a congregation that had formed to spare people living in that part of the township from having to make the long drive to the old church which had been built (and rebuilt several times) by Ickka and her generation of Lutheran settlers.

In time, though, the Buss-Flessner children began drifting further away. Land in South Prairie had all been taken. The price of developed land was high and showed no signs of ever becoming cheaper or cheap enough for young people to buy without family help. Ickka had done her part, but that wasn't enough to satisfy the wants of all her offspring. Fortunately, cheap land was still available in other parts of Illinois, and it could be had for the asking in the new state of Nebraska.

Heinrich was the first of Ickka's blood to leave. Hoag, Nebraska was his destination, a place which would become another center for those of Ostfriesen heritage.

Through all of this the grandchildren sprouted up, and little Wilhelmina Catharina, who Ickka had been so proud to see walk down the aisle in her confirmation dress, was the first to appear there in satin and lace. This time Ickka may have had tears in her eyes. After that, the next wave of marriages among grandchildren came fast and furious, time seeming to compress for Ickka, each year almost flashing before her eyes even as her body slowed down and became crippled with arthritis.

In 1897, after twenty-two years together, Ickka's second husband, Heinrich Mimke Flessner died. This followed the death by typhoid of her oldest son, Gerhard, and the effective loss of his entire family as his widow, Anna, took her children and moved them to the Hoag, Nebraska's Ostfriesen community.

Even with all these people absent Ickka was seldom alone after Heinrich's death. Tradition said that she should live with her one remaining daughter, but that would mean leaving the vast majority of her descendants behind and moving to Pike County where Jenny now lived … something she felt was out of the question. Even worse, it would force her to abandon her church, her friends, and her position as the leading matron of her community.

Ickka had become an institution, known for her pioneering and her farming as far away as the county seat in Quincy where people spoke of her with respect and where she was considered one of the most influential German-Americans of her generation in her township. If you wanted something done in Clayton Township or to know how to go about getting it done, Ickka Buss-Flessner was the go-to person. Not that she engaged in politics. She didn't. But age and her involvement in the development of community, church, and farming since the area's settlement made her the most knowledgeable person around. Plus, she was not free with her opinions with the result that, when she spoke, people listened.

So she did not follow custom when Heinrich died. She would

visit Jenny to see her grandchildren, but she would not move to Kinderhook. Besides, she'd become attached to her home—the house her second husband had built for his first wife.

Ickka lived on until 1908, dying at the age of eighty-six only ten years before her great-granddaughter, Marolyn, would be born to Jenny's youngest son, who was also the youngest of Ickka's sixteen Miller-Buss grandchildren.

What happened to her estate? Over her lifetime she'd bought and sold land parcels varying in price from $4,000 to $800. She'd made considerable amounts during the Civil War and Reconstruction. Some of her profits were plowed back into land and more land, then redeemed as more profit. Since she died intestate and documents on the estate dispersal seem to have been lost in the bowels of time, we can't even guess at the remaining total. Whatever it was, it would have been divided between the surviving children with the offspring of her deceased children splitting their shares. Thus, Janna would've received 1/7th share of whatever.

Her obituary in the local newspaper gives an idea of how she was seen in her later years:

…It was then [following Jann's death, she] … had a fierce struggle for life fighting in behalf of herself and her flock of little ones the battles on the wild prairies. But with childlike confidence and trust in her Lord she struggled bravely on till success crowned her efforts. … Her pew will be vacant and her familiar figure and especially her cordial sincere counsel and assistance will be sorely missed by her pastor and her people. … She passed away … lamented by one daughter, four sons, forty-six grandchildren, fifty-nine great grandchildren, and many other relatives and numerous friends …" *Golden New Era*, July 2, 1908

22
The Transition Years – Sena

*…what a wonderful, kind, sweet lady she was; she had the most
nearly unflawed character of anybody I have known…*
Richard Armstrong, Jr., grandson 1975

Most of the older Miller children left home individually to attend college, one or more being gone at any one time. But when Sena's turn came, Chris decided to send the younger boys along with her to Jacksonville thereby clearing the house of children with one sharp break. Mary, who had returned home to help with the youngsters and who had mellowed into a spinster lady, went along as a housekeeper and surrogate mother. And so the years passed in a new pattern for Mary, Sena, Walter, and young Willie—winters in Jacksonville with wide circles of mainstream American friends, sports, academics, and all in English. Walter was in high school; Willie in grade school. Sena thrived as a college student, and they all enjoyed summers back on the farm and holidays visiting other members of the family.

Grandpa Hermann Miller, though, was no longer with them, having passed away in Quincy, as already noted. Shortly thereafter, Bertha moved to Kinderhook to live with Chris and Jenny—all of whom were now experiencing the "empty nest" syndrome. That is, while their big house was far from empty, it no longer echoed with the clatter of children during the winter months. Summers were different.

Time rolled back during the hot season with the younger Millers home for the school vacation. Chris and his twin brothers had, of course, invested in the latest in farming technology (such as it was), but the land remained labor intensive, and men and boys alike worked outside from dawn to dinner, the younger Millers growing up during those short summer months much as their ancestors had. Thus, Walter and Willie (now being called "Billy" by some because his friends said he was as stubborn as a billy goat) helped with everything from plowing to harvesting, while Sena's hands and knees developed calluses scouring the floors. All of the women pitched in at keeping the big coal range in the kitchen stoked with coal and free from ash, scalding chicken carcasses to remove the pinfeathers, churning butter, putting up preserves, boiling clothes on wash day, using the coal-heated iron on ironing day, and sharing secrets for preparing delicious foods like Jenny's biscuits, for one, they all swore were the best in the state. When they weren't working in the house, the women were outside in Jenny's garden, which was big enough to supply a winter's worth of food and required hours of attention every day.

Yet, there was time for laughter, too. It floated around the big Kinderhook house or in nearby Hull as the extended family gathered in the evenings for games like charades and 'murder in the dark,' the language shifting from English to Plattdeutsch. Hochdeutsch, now just called German, was completely foreign to these young Millers. It was not spoken at home or at school or, even, at church. In fact, it had become so unfamiliar that the youngest of the Millers, would struggle to get even average grades when he took it as a second language in college.

Whatever the language, there was time for just sitting around the kitchen table or the long dining room table or out on the front porch. Fireflies flickered in shrubs and trees, crickets and frogs sang their evening songs and the family added their voices, talking about the events of the day. Theodore Roosevelt was in the White House for most of this period, ushering in "progressivism" and an era which saw the growth of American power. The "great white fleet" of twelve mighty naval warships set off to sail around the world, its massive firepower a muscle-flexing message to foreign capitals that there was a new kid on the block. New laws seemed to sprout from nowhere, laws aimed at cleaning up the notorious Chicago stockyards, at getting sawdust out of cereals, at regulating the preparation and sale of drugs.

Then, too, the family was learning new terminology, like conservationism, protectionism, American exceptionalism, and American ingenuity. The newspapers also brought a weekly diet of current issues to explore. Did society have a responsibility to care for its weakest members? Should women get the vote? Was capitalism America's proper answer to European socialism? How much control should the government exert over private business?

Well, regardless their views on these topics, they could all feel comfortable berating the big industrialists and the trade unions, blaming them for misfortunes like the market crash of 1907 in which Chris lost a fair amount of money.

The subjects under discussion changed slightly from year to year. When 1910 rolled around, Sena graduated Phi Beta Kappa. Howard Taft was in the White House now while, judging by her accomplishments, Sena might well be headed there. She could look back on four years during which she'd been on the debate team, had served as vice president of the classes of 1906-10, and been elected vice-president of the Philomathian Literary

Sena Marie and Mary Miller

Society (1907-1908). She'd also been a member of the Rambler Board (*The Rambler* was the college newspaper) in 1909-1910 and the recipient of the Smith Prize (mathematics) in 1908, the Ireland Prize (philosophy), and the Elizabeth Delano Ames Prize in 1909.

Were these to be the best years of her life? Had she reached the pinnacle of female accomplishment? Was she now supposed to go off and teach snot-nosed kids in some rural Illinois schoolhouse? Of course, she could marry. She was pretty and could cook and sew and, maybe—just maybe—some good Ostfriesen-American boy would be willing to overlook her education. Sena wanted none of this. She had no interest in spending her life as a drudge, even as a gilded drudge like her mother. She'd seen that life and had no intention of going backwards in time.

"Women everywhere are doing great things," she no doubt heard over and over. "You can, too." Young women had been flooding into the cities for several decades and finding work there. She could, too. But it'd be better if she had more education. But, graduate school for a woman? That was still unusual.

Chris Miller, though, liked the idea. The world was changing so fast. His beautiful daughter would face challenges unknown to his mother and grandmother, and Sena had the brains to not only hang onto the tiger's tail but to ride the beast. He wanted to help her do just that.

Chris had had a ringside seat to economic, social, and political upheavals on a scale unknown in the prior history of mankind. To name but a few: moving picture theaters appeared; Henry Ford implemented the first assembly line; men sent voice and picture signals over landlines; national parks were created; labor unions matured; Susan B. Anthony and her sisters revolutionized the nation's social conscience; and *Montgomery Ward* and *Sears Roebuck* catalogs made a sea change in the world's buying habits. Imagine. A person could purchase anything—even a house— through the mail. Machines were appearing everywhere, even in the farm and in the house.

There was more. Much more. Cities now had "trolley car" suburbs, and a Chicago architect figured out how to engineer a sky scraper. Within a decade, cities everywhere began pushing into the skies. The world had elevators to deliver people up to "sky walks" while the miraculous "Ferris Wheel" took others around and around through the air. The Panama Canal, another engineering marvel, had opened, and a transportation network of rail and some 3,500 miles of road laced across the nation. Most people rode the trains, but everyone was buying Ford's Model T and the new Automobile Club was putting signs on roads. And, marvel of marvels, man could even fly.

Social change accompanied this and, where social change was no new phenomenon to humans, before it had been a slow process, had been something a person could get used to along the way, not something that required rapid and radical adjustment. But this time? Industrialization changed the economic order, gobbling up men, women and children in its factories. The result to the social order? By 1910, the average child living in an inner city was malnourished, and child mortality rates were abominable. Women had few rights, domestic abuse was common, divorce was rare unless sought by the husband, most jobs open to women were at salaries less than half of a man's, and—at that—the average annual wage for an America male was only $750 a year. Oh, yes. Change was coming. It had to.

Very little of this proved relevant or even noticeable back among the Ostfriesen-Americans of Golden and South Prairie or even to those who'd moved to new communities in Nebraska. They still rode or drove horses for transportation or used their own God-given two feet. Horses and oxen pulled plows. Men wielded sickles as they had in the old country or walked behind primitive swathers. They heated their houses with wood and coal and went to bed with the sun. Jenny's older brothers continued to posit their important issues in terms of land values and crops, of whether English or German should be the language of the church, of how much education a woman would need. "Enough to be able to handle the egg money" was still the general consensus. Although no one begrudged the occasional girl from getting enough learning to become a school teacher. After all, not every girl could be expected to find a respectable man to wed.

Chris' older daughters had adhered closely enough to the pattern to continue to fit in back among their cousins in South Prairie. But Sena?

What about Sena?

What made her different? Was it just her experience at Illinois College and the influence of her instructors? Or did it go further back—perhaps to her sixth year when Chris loaded up the family and, like over 700,000 other Americans, took one of the hundreds of trains that carried them into Chicago for the 1893 Chicago World's Fair. It was a "once-in-a-lifetime" event that no one could miss. It was the "Great White City" of some 200 buildings erected on the banks of Lake Michigan and containing every marvel the world then knew or could invent for the occasion, like Ferris's giant wheel and the massive Women's Exposition Building, a three-story structure designed by a woman architect and commissioned by Chicago's Board of Lady Managers, its interior fully decorated by women artisans and artists.

No one went away disappointed. They all agreed. The fair-going experience was magical, so much so that it proved the inspiration for Frank Baum's "Wizard of Oz" series. And the effect of a week in this paradise on a little girl?

Was Sena one of the 2,000 people a day who had tea in the rooftop café of the Women's Building? Maybe she was perched on the edge of her seat at the Wild West Show when Annie Oakley performed her amazing shooting acts or when Buffalo Bill Cody galloped his white horse across the arena, his own white hair streaming behind him, to slide to a stop in front of a box holding a small, elderly woman in a black suit embroidered with red flowers. Did she see the legendary Colonel Cody bow deeply and Susan B. Anthony rise to her feet to flutter a handkerchief in acknowledgement as the sell-out crowd roared approval? Sena wouldn't have recognized the significance of the moment then, but she may have carried it with her. Susan B. certainly became one of her abiding role models.

Perhaps the memory of those moments remained with Sena when she applied to the University of Chicago graduate school of history with the idea of taking her master's degree and becoming a college instructor. If so, she was in luck that she had a supportive father with a comfortable income, which made it all quite easy.

The University of Chicago provided exactly the environment she wanted and needed. Founded only twenty years previously, it welcomed women students, even in its graduate programs, and had already matriculated women who were making a mark on society. When Sena walked through its gates that Fall of 1910, she certainly knew she was following in very large footsteps. These were made by women like Edith and Grace Abbott who had come from near poverty in Nebraska. Each had struggled to work their way through undergraduate school and into the University of Chicago's graduate programs—Edith getting her PhD in Economics in 1905 and Grace her PhM in Social Science in 1909. Both had lived at Chicago's Hull House, which was a residence for women as well as ministering to the poor.

Sena knew all about Edith and Grace and may have met them. At this point, though, she was not thinking so much about reforming society as about just getting her master's in history. So, in the summer of 1910, Chris Miller took the train up to Chicago to settle his daughter. His oldest daughter, Lena, was then living in Chicago's Ward 6, not far from the University, and it's likely that Chris took Sena to her. Lena, whose husband was a medical doctor at this point, had only one child who was then in her teens and, certainly, would not have considered the idea of boarding her younger sister as an imposition. Possibly, Chris found something else for her, Chicago being full of "women's residences" designed to safely accommodate single women.

On the other hand, maybe not. Only thirteen years had passed since the notorious serial killer, H.H. Holmes, had been executed for luring his victims to him by building and running a Chicago residential hotel for women. A proven number of six women had been tortured and killed there. The true number, however, was unknowable and could have reached—the tabloid press said it had certainly reached—two hundred. While Holmes had been summarily dealt with by the State of Illinois, you could never know if there weren't copycats out there. After all, Holmes had literally gotten away with murder for a very long time.

Thus, we can imagine Chris played it safe and lodged Sena comfortably with Dr. and Mrs. William E. Brenneman while the boys and Mary returned to Jacksonville for the school year.

Three months later this all changed. Chris rented a house in Chicago, jerked his younger boys out of schools in Jacksonville after the Christmas break, and shipped them and Mary to Chicago, enrolling both boys at the University of Chicago (young Willie in the university's high school). Sena, of course, moved in with them, and the old gang was back together.

Still and all, why? We can speculate. It might've had nothing to do with Sena at all. Chris might simply have decided that the expense of maintaining Mary and the boys in Jacksonville and Sena in Chicago was too great. It's possible that he may have suffered one of his financial reversals at this time.

On the other hand, Lena may have found Sena just too much of a handful and a poor role model for her own daughter. We can almost hear her saying: "I don't approve, and she just won't listen to me!"

Certainly, Sena began immersing herself in the society and activities of Chicago's rather radical social reformers almost immediately after beginning at the University of Chicago. Just as she had in Jacksonville, she joined clubs and attended meetings. Except now the nature of these changed. She raised her voice in social advocacy and marched in demonstrations. She wrote leaflets and picketed city hall. This may even have been the college term when she managed to get herself arrested and jailed during a suffragette demonstration, an event that did happen at some point during these first years in Chicago and which she described to me with a smile a half a century later. A night in jail would have brought Chris to Chicago in a hurry and, certainly, provided a reason for the abrupt changes in living arrangements.

All that said, we shouldn't overlook the possibility that it might have been a romantic attachment that Chris felt unsuitable? Sena was drawn to society's underdogs and, while Chris was a liberal, there was a line he wouldn't have willingly allowed Sena to cross. In his world unmarried women were still legally and morally the charge of their fathers.

Whatever happened, Chris did not renege on his promise to put Sena through graduate school. He simply changed her living arrangements and gave her a different chaperone. Mary.

Big sister Mary was no intellectual slouch, herself, and she undoubtedly welcomed the move from Jacksonville's small college cultural environment to the big city. Being 'Mom,' of course, meant a full-time job of cooking and cleaning. Chris found a house for his children near the campus and most likely equipped it with such conveniences as had trickled into the domestic sphere during the industrial revolution.

"Modern" Chicago homes of this decade included electric lights, running water, central heating, and a water closet with a commode. Mary's kitchen definitely had the normal city amenities of a coal-burning range, and the house would've been equipped with a coal cellar accessed by an outside door. Another modern convenience was her icebox with a handsome wood exterior, a zinc interior, and a hollow core full of cork insulation. A drip pan sat under it while a door in its back gave out to the back porch and was used by the iceman to replenish the ice supply on his daily rounds.

Mary's day included reminding the boys about carrying coal up from the cellar and splitting wood to start her fires. The boys would also be charged with carrying ash out to an ash dump and emptying the icebox's drip tray. Still, even without those chores, she would spend over fifty percent of her waking hours in the kitchen. Then, there would be one day a week devoted to the washing, another day to the ironing and mending, and hours out of every day to cleaning—the coal dust from her stove and from the tens of thousands of fires in all the high-rise apartments and tenements and low-rise suburbs and slums making it nearly impossible to keep a house clean. Chicago was a very dirty city.

These labors left Mary with little time to go out to enjoy the cultural advantages of the city or the social and political ferment sweeping the campus. Still, she doubtless made time, catching a trolley car to the city's major attractions, enjoying the museums during the occasional day trip and concerts and the theater on the rare nighttime excursion—of course, accompanied by her siblings. Then, too, the younger Millers brought friends and new ideas home with them.

Walter was in his final year of undergraduate school, studying geology. He, even more than Sena, was considered the brains in the family but that might have had as much to do with his gender as his mental prowess. Willie was attending the University of Chicago's high school where he was an average student. No one ever thought he would set the academic world on fire, being more likely to sketch along the edges of his papers than to pen anything erudite. But both boys were tall and good-looking and made friends among their new peers, Walter much more readily than Willie who tended to be a bit aloof.

Besides, he had little interest in social or any other kind of reform. His Chicago was a city of art galleries, theaters, and music. Hermann's violin, that very old instrument Hermann had carried with him from Bühren, had come to Willie after Hermann's death, and he loved it. For a time he thought about becoming a professional musician, playing in a student orchestra and a string quartet and saving his money for much treasured tickets to concerts. Finally, he got a job ushering at the new Chicago Opera House and, thereafter, could indulge his passion while earning a bit of money.

The Miller kitchen became a gathering place for various groups of students and for heated discussions rising not just from social change but from economic and political developments within and without America. It wasn't only in Chicago where young people saw the need for change but everywhere. The young Millers were, indeed, living in interesting times.

Everything and anything seemed possible to them and their peer group at the University. The Russian Revolution was sweeping out the old order. The European monarchies with all the remnants of feudalism were going or gone. Various -isms were being conceptualized and matured—socialism, communism, Marxism, anarchism, all those -isms that would cause so much trouble in the end. But for the moment? It was heady stuff.

"We met. We talked. We argued and debated and read and wrote," Sena would say to me many years later. "But that wasn't enough. We felt we had to put our ideas into action, so we lobbied and campaigned and we took our causes to the streets and marched. To be a woman in graduate school at Chicago meant you were part of something huge, something that could be earthshattering. We thought of ourselves as revolutionaries and reformers."

Chris probably didn't intend to rein in Sena's activism. Nor is it likely he minded exposing his youngest boys to the same influences. The social ferment of the time was irresistible, and Chris wasn't the sort of father who would deny his children their opportunity to be part of historical change. Of them all, though, it was Sena who took advantage of her father's liberalism and her own relative freedom. Early in her Chicago experience she'd begun modeling herself on the Abbott sisters.

Grace Abbott was a power at Hull House, and by 1910 Edith Abbott was making a name for herself as an educator, a career which would eventually bring her back to the city as the first dean of Chicago's School of Social Service Administration and the first American woman to be dean of any graduate school.

Another huge influence on Sena's life was a woman named Grace Trout—the Chicago organizer of the women's emancipation movement in Illinois. Grace began by participating in marches and parades, but then she came up with an even better idea. Why not take Chicago demonstrations to communities across the state? To that end she organized the more important and better known women among the suffragettes, persuaded them to donate automobiles and to form a motorcade. They would go from town to town, stopping to talk to local politicians, lobbying them on their own turf, taking the message to women in their homes.

It wasn't easy. They carried their own petrol and tire patch kits and water and spare parts. Roads were primitive to non-existent. Lodging was mostly in homes that opened to accept them, but in many places they were distinctly not welcome. They were feted in some towns and pelted with rotten tomatoes in others and, sometimes, both at the same time.

This and other activism, though, worked. In 1913 the Illinois state legislature gave the women of Illinois the right to vote in state and local elections.

But long before that happened, Mary began suffering stomach aches which she passed off as nothing. Persuaded to see a doctor, she was diagnosed with a bowel obstruction, one which could be removed with surgery. Without surgery, she was told, it would probably kill her.

True or not, Mary was convinced and had the procedure. Everyone in the family must've known and shuddered at the risks. And their worst fears were realized. The 40-year-old woman, who had been both big sister and mother to the younger Millers, passed out of their lives due to 'post-surgical complications,' probably peritonitis.

Her role as housekeeper for the boys now fell to Sena. It was impossible to both maintain a house, keep up with her classes, and continue her social welfare activities. That summer she dropped out of her graduate program. Walter was 21 now and took his undergraduate degree that spring. Willie was 15 and going into his junior year of high school.

For the next five years Sena kept house for her brothers but in a much reduced way. The boys no longer got a free ride but learned to do their own ironing and mending. Unlike Mary, Sena had work to do. It might have been volunteer work, but she was serious about it. In the mornings she would tie up her long hair, wrapping it in roles that circled her head, would secure a hat on top with long, deadly, pearl-headed pins and would march out the door—literally marching when there were marches. Into the street she'd go with her friends and fellow conspirators while wind howled through Chicago's canyons tearing at skirts that became a bit shorter every year.

With money saved from the household allowance, she rode the Chicago El to committee meetings and traveled to outlying neighborhoods where she went door to door canvasing householders, drumming up support for a laundry list of causes, not the least of which was national suffrage for women. In the meantime Walter was in graduate school studying Geology and Paleontology, while Willie had graduated from high school, spent a couple of terms at Chicago, decided he didn't like it (and his grades showed it), and enrolled at the Chicago Art Institute without informing his father.

Willie's move to the Art Institute brought about another weather change for the family. He opened up another world and brought into their home a new group with a different view of the times.

"They call that period the Chicago Renaissance," Sena would tell me. It was a period that many saw as the beginning of a new Chicago—one with a soul and a culture. There was an explosion of thought-provoking writing and new forms of art and everyone seemed to be involved in some cause or another. As Sena said, "There just seemed to be so much to do, so many changes needed, and a sense of all being involved together. Now they call it social ferment. At the time it certainly felt like ferment. We were going to create the perfect world, one person and one reform at a time."

Which brought George Angerstein into her life.

Sena was twenty-five when she met this extraordinary young lawyer from southern Illinois. He lived with a crippling form of arthritis that affects the young and that he'd had since early childhood. He hadn't let it slow him down, though, and getting around on two canes, he donated as much time as he could spare to social causes, his path crossing Sena's with some frequency, both working as volunteers and donating what small amounts of cash they could spare to the poor and disadvantaged. George, of course, was also building his legal practice.

Given his physical handicap, it took him some time before he felt comfortable pressing a romantic suit on a woman as attractive and accomplished as Sena even though there was nothing bashful about this aggressive young man. In 1916, George and Sena married. They would have two children. George would go on to become a successful attorney and a modest philanthropist.

With the marriage, Sena moved into yet another social and economic bracket, she and George becoming part of Chicago's young married reformers set. She bore two children, managed a household with servants, entertained her husband's clients, got her children into good schools, and … then … Sena went back to graduate school. This time she studied under her role model Edith Abbott, spending a year learning more about effective ways of enacting social service legislation and administering social services. In the Angerstein household from this time on, George would make the money; Sena would set it to doing good.

Then came World War I, the roaring twenties, and the birth of Ickka's great granddaughter, Marolyn— the new pioneer and the subject of Volume II of "Determined Women." Read on …

Marolyn Dale Miller

ACKNOWLEDGEMENTS

Thanks to my now friend and cousin by marriage, Debi Baum, this book is a reality. Her help and encouragement were vital to and inspired big hunks of it. She was unfailingly generous with her time and assistance while her book *The Buss Family of Ostfriesland* along with another family genealogy, *Der Muellers Sohn: An Ostfrisian and American Family in Historical Context*, by Dennis D. Miller, were my bibles. *When the Wind Blows* by Anna Wienke was a wonderful resource on Golden's history. Carl Landrum's *Historical Sketches of Quincy Illinois* did the same for Quincy, while my copy of Robert H. Behrens *We Will Go to a New Land: The Great East Frisian Migration to America 1845-1895* is replete with highlighted passages I tried to memorize.

Other contributions came from: Jean Kay, the research historian at the Historical Society of Quincy and Adams County, Kenneth Flesner, president of the Golden Historical Society, publications from the Ostfriesen Genealogical Society of America, helpful librarians at the Quincy and Berwyn, Illinois public libraries, and personnel at the United States Forest Service Wapiti District office. Nomie Budelier, a German linguist/genealogist and former colleague, led me to various sources on the minutiae of life in nineteenth century Germany. Tina Meinen and her mother, Minna, both of Buhren, Germany, reviewed the Mueller chapters and provided helpful information and photos. Larry Haschemeyer, a Golden historian, was generous with photos and background documents and in providing a tour of Golden and its environs. Elizabeth Koutny of Berwyn was kind enough to show me around her home (an identical twin of the Smith/Miller house next door).

Then, there's the internet and Google. Maps and dozens of tidbits came from Google internet searches, including translation services and references to pertinent articles—like Dr. John Saathoof's *The Ostfriesians in America*. The internet also yielded fact checks to augment my memory, on-line articles by the Bureau of Reclamation on the Shoshone Project, being just one example.

No acknowledgement involving any of my writing projects is complete without mention of my daughter, Robyn McGuckin, whose encouragement kept me working on the necessary writing skills long after I might otherwise have given up.

Thank you all.

February 2014

CPSIA information can be obtained
at www.ICGtesting.com
Printed in the USA
LVHW031116200319
611264LV00002B/357/P

9 780990 872726